THE WORD TO SET YOU FREE

✤ *The Word* ✤
to Set You Free

Living Faith and
Biblical Criticism

—

DAVID BROWN

First published in Great Britain 1995
Society for Promoting Christian Knowledge
Holy Trinity Church
Marylebone Road
London NW1 4DU

© David Brown 1995

British Library Cataloguing-in-Publication Data
A catalogue record for this book is available from the British Library

ISBN 0-281-04806-1

Typeset by Dorwyn Ltd, Rowlands Castle, Hants
Printed in Great Britain by
The Cromwell Press, Melksham, Wilts

CONTENTS

—

CONTENTS

Conclusion: SPREADING THE GOSPEL

Introduction
How to use this book

—

Over the past two centuries our understanding of the Bible has been revolutionized by detailed analysis of how its various books came to be written. Commonly called 'biblical criticism', this can often cause alarm in the minds and hearts of ordinary believers, as though it were all a matter of 'criticizing' the Bible in various ways for not being true. Where then is faith, it is asked. Where is there something reliable in which to put our trust? But there is really no need for such worry. Just as we can find the film, television, or art critic helpful in guiding our understanding and appreciation of what we see, so in principle can the same also be true of the biblical critic.

Unfortunately, until relatively recently (in common with many other arts subjects) biblical studies has been in the grip of a rather narrow pursuit of scientific objectivity, of trying to discover 'the facts' (When was something written? How reliable is it historically? How has it been modified through the process of oral or written transmission? etc.) rather than with identifying what significance these facts might have for us today. This in turn has filtered into the churches, with the minister or priest perplexed as to how he or she might relate biblical studies to everyday life, and thus thinking one thing in the study and presenting quite another in the pulpit. Perhaps this partly explains the brevity of many sermons today, with preachers afraid of being caught out in their own internal tensions! At all events, the result is a community of faith which still, more often than not, regards the pronouncements of biblical scholarship with suspicion.

That too was my experience when I first studied theology; and so when I became a priest, I determined that – no matter how difficult it should prove – I would attempt to integrate fully these two areas of my life: study and pulpit. To my delight this seemed to enable me to communicate the good news of Jesus Christ *more* effectively, not less. But this should not have surprised me, for the biblical writers themselves had thought spiritual significance more important than a literal recording of events. It was this that had enabled them to speak so powerfully to their own generation, and in effect made their writings like a series of sermons – and only secondarily, if at all, history. It was not that history was unimportant, but it remained rightly subordinate to symbol, to conveying religious truth. Through acknowledging this, the text ceased to be a burden upon me; instead it insisted that I too spoke of God's power of healing and renewal for my own day.

The chapters that follow were originally precisely this: attempts to communicate that insight through the vehicle of the pulpit. Each sermon, however, has been rewritten, so that the book can now be used in one of two ways: either continuously, or as a series of meditations to which one might return at intervals. If the latter method is employed, then the indices should prove especially helpful if one wants to see how a particular biblical passage is treated, or pursue a particular theme (such as salvation, suffering, doubt, or other faiths), as the topic is periodically taken up through the course of the book. If read continuously, then readers will observe from the contents page that Part Two takes them through the history of Israel, beginning at the Garden of Eden and ending in the second century BC with Daniel, while Part Three proceeds similarly with respect to the life of Christ: beginning by setting the scene, and ending with his resurrection. Part One is intended as introductory, with various analogies provided which, it is hoped, will not only make more palatable the notion of a fallible Bible but help the reader to view this fact as part of the wonderful generosity and providential love of God as our creator.

To reject parts of the Bible as morally repugnant, and even some aspects of a particular Gospel as theologically inadequate, may initially sound like the height of human arrogance. But the preacher like the ordinary believer lives as part of a community of faith, and what must surely ultimately determine our perceptions is not isolated verses, but the received wisdom of that community as it has developed over the centuries. So while (as I shall attempt to demonstrate) biblical studies can often throw up new and challenging readings for us that will deepen our faith, it can also at times demand a reading which it is only proper we should declare illustrates the all too fallible character of the writer concerned. The test must be what best fits into the picture of our faith as a whole. That is why, unlike the professional biblical scholar, I never treat the Old Testament on its own. For the Christian its reading must be related to what comes after, and that is why not only is Part Two called 'Gospel Anticipations' but also each meditation within it is concerned to relate what was originally said to how we might live as Christians today.

A sermon meditation is hardly the place to introduce the technical language of biblical studies. Therefore, although what is known respectively as textual, source, form, redaction, narrative, and canonical criticism all occur, and thus by the end of the book the reader will know implicitly quite a lot about such methods and results, none of these (with the exception of the first) is so designated by name. Instead, they are allowed to emerge almost incidentally since for me the whole point in using them is to enhance the good news that is the gospel. We now know that the conventions of the ancient world allowed a freedom in relation to historical fact that is quite unlike our own. Almost a millennium later (in the Book of Leviticus), Moses is still commandeered to say things to a society radically different from his own, just as Matthew and Luke adapt Jesus' words with the same purpose in view, while John even goes a stage further – in ascribing whole discourses to Jesus that were almost certainly never uttered. The aim in all such cases was to communicate a greater truth: that is, how the distant past can still impact upon the reader's present. That, in my view, is something that the writers of both the Old and the

New Testaments do quite brilliantly. Books like Deuteronomy or John become more impressive, not less, and they are certainly not to be despised because of their very loose relation to history. Rather, the preacher's task is to ensure that that process of application continues. Jesus is not just a figure of the past, but our risen and living Lord who can transform lives in the here and now.

Whether I have succeeded in making credible how this process of writing works is for the reader to judge. Certainly, for me, such an approach to the Bible has led to no diminution of faith. I can say the two historic creeds in their traditional sense without qualms, and in the course of what follows the reader will find me speaking in defence of miracles, virgin birth and empty tomb. Some in consequence will find what I say too conservative. Yet there will be many others who suppose that 'orthodoxy' of itself must involve a commitment to endorse and defend 'truth' in Scripture, even where it has been effectively undermined either by the work of the historian or by the subsequent moral or spiritual judgement of the Church. To all such the words of John's Jesus stand as a perpetual challenge: 'the truth will make you free' (John 8.32 RSV). By insisting that only adherence to the literal truth of the words of the Bible could achieve this, they achieve a splendid irony. For, if we look up the context (discussed in chapter 33) what we find is that it is part of an argument against the Jews' reliance upon the dead weight of the past. The past in itself can only destroy, not give life. It is the Word as the source of all existence and life (John 8. 58) that brings life in all its fullness, true liberty. It is my earnest prayer that the words that follow will entice my readers away from a literal (but dead) past, and draw them instead towards the living Word: the Word to set them free.

Special thanks are due to Tim Perry for creating a beautifully word-processed order out of my untidy, not to say chaotic, manuscript. I am also very grateful to two friends, Ann Loades and David Fuller, for their consistent encouragement, and helpful comments on the manuscript. So many versions of Scripture are now in use that I have allowed what follows to reflect that diversity. Though the majority of quotations come from the *Revised Standard Version* (RSV), use has also been made of the *Authorized Version* (AV), *The New English Bible* (NEB), the *Jerusalem Bible* (JB), *Today's English Version* (TEV), and the Book of Common Prayer (BCP); very occasionally, I have offered my own translation.

✤ Part One ✤
The Revealer at Work

1 ✤ *The God with Dirty Hands*

—

[Mary] gave birth to her first-born son . . . and laid him in a manger
(Luke 2. 7 RSV)

Were you to see a talk advertised on the theme of 'The God with Dirty Hands', you could easily be forgiven for thinking that what was on offer was yet another attack upon Christianity, with its God denied a clean slate and apparently justly condemned because of all the suffering and cruelty which exists in the world. But ironically that same title, when taken literally, can also be used to point to Christianity's appropriate response, and it is with that response and how it affects our understanding of the Bible that I want now to engage.

Many other contemporary theologians have made quite clear their lack of interest in Jesus' infancy and early adulthood. For them the first few chapters of Matthew and Luke are simply mythological equivalents of what is expressed metaphysically, and more profoundly, in the opening chapter of John. I could not disagree more. For all the profundity of his Gospel, John's Jesus passes too easily, too confidently, too triumphantly, through this world, and in my view what liberal and conservative alike need to hear with greater urgency is what it must have meant for God to have taken human form amidst all the ambiguities implied by the infancy narratives.

In his sermons, Martin Luther makes much of the paradox of God being suckled at Mary's breasts. Of course, it would be very easy to turn this into a cloying image, but the truth behind it is of vital import: that God in the incarnation made himself utterly

3

dependent on human beings as he grew to adulthood, not least on the qualities of Mary and Joseph as parents. Not only that, he subjected himself to all the normal limitations of a child being brought up in a peasant's home in first-century Palestine, with all the inadequacies of education and accommodation which that implied. And here we return to the God with dirty hands. 'Manger' in Luke 2.7 may well have meant that Jesus was laid in the feeding trough for the animals, but whether so or not, their inevitable dirt would never have been far distant from his play as a child since, just like crofts in the Scottish Highland even as recently as this century, human beings and animals in the normal home in first-century Palestine were accustomed to living under the same roof, often with only a low wall between them.

Then there were all those years of learning by trial and error his trade as a carpenter. To suppose that it was a nice little comfortable family business is, I suspect, once more to err from the reality. Perhaps we need to be shocked into the truth as was *The Times* art critic in 1850 when he saw John Everett Millais's painting of 'Christ in the House of his Parents', now in the Tate Gallery in London. His column read: 'The attempt to associate the holy family with the meanest of details of a carpenter's shop, with no conceivable omission of misery, of dirt, of even disease, all finished with the same loathsome minuteness, is disgusting.' But, loathsome or not, it is precisely that kind of God of which the infancy narratives speak; it is no saccharine playtoy, but a God born amidst the muck of a byre, and with dirty, calloused hands as he sought to help his own poor family make ends meet. Indeed, with Sepphoris, the provincial capital of Galilee, only three miles distant from Nazareth, might we not envisage Jesus working there as an ordinary labourer, and even queuing up in the hope of being employed at Tiberias, the new capital that was being built to replace it after AD 18?

The God with dirty hands is thus surely no misnomer, but why mention this? The answer is that it seems to me to provide the proper clue to understanding both the way our world is, and

God's answer to it. Neither the fundamentalist nor the liberal is right. God neither drops us the blueprint from heaven, nor does he leave it all up to us. Rather, he gets his hands dirty. Because of the value he attaches to our free response, he engages with the community of faith in a way that allows it (and us) space in coming to a proper understanding, and that means the space for misunderstanding as much as understanding, the throwing of our own dirt back at him. That is why the Bible is this strange mixture of the sublime and the ridiculous, the wicked and the transcendently good. For how else are we to reconcile the beauty and the muck we find so often lying side by side – as, for instance, in Psalm 137, which lyrically describes worship of God in a foreign land, only to end with an appalling, blood-curdling expression of desire to destroy one's enemy's children ('dash them against the stones'), or in the Book of Revelation, with its marvellous account of the New Jerusalem uttered in the same breath as the great mass of humanity is assigned to torment and perdition?

Yet to say that is to give only half the story. For the God of whom we speak engaged with us not just at a distance in the words of the Bible, but himself directly as the Word Incarnate in all the ambiguities which we ourselves experience as we search after God or seek to respond to him. Thus, as passages like Mark 3.31–35 and 6.1–6 make all too clear, Jesus himself was initially (and for some time) misunderstood by his mother and family; so even those closest to him were of no help. Again, making that misunderstanding all the more intelligible, he himself appears only gradually to have fully understood the nature of his mission. Thus there is much argument among scholars over the precise point at which he accepted his vocation as Messiah, or whether indeed he ever even saw himself in such terms. Then what about his understanding of the Gentile world? Some suggest that it took the sharpness of his conversation with the Syro-Phoenician woman over what might be given to Gentile dogs (Mark 7.24–30) to awaken in him a value for the Gentiles not hitherto acknowledged within the Jewish tradition. Obviously such issues as these are too complex to enter into here. Suffice it to note that both the temptations and the cross itself well indicate a self-understanding not easily won. For in his temptations we see how even miracles did not escape the ambiguities of human existence. Jesus asks, might they do no more than show him a mere social reformer or stunt man? Then again on the cross he cries the agonized cry of all sufferers, 'My God, my God, why have you forsaken me?' and only gradually comes to acceptance. Little wonder then that the disciples only fully understood who this man was after the resurrection.

The basic point that I want to make is, I hope, now clear. The splendour and the muck which generally characterize our world are no less true not only of the Bible, but of the very life of God incarnate. The muck of the byre in which he was born, the calloused hands with which he laboured, the spit of the soldiers which dribbled down his tortured face, all speak of a God who so completely identified with the human condition that our struggles, sorrows, and disappointments became his own. The dirt thrown in God's face has become the dirt on his hands, through which he can carry us beyond to his own greater purposes for us.

2 ✤ The Good Teacher and the Wise Parent

—

It was I who taught Ephraim to walk
(Hosea 11.3 RSV)

In trying to understand the character of revelation, analogies can sometimes help. As we shall see, both of those which I am about to suggest are employed within Scripture itself. Consider first the occupation in which I myself am employed, that of teacher. Those familiar with that profession will, I'm sure, all have heard (or will hear at some time in their lives) as a rationale of education the fact that its Latin root means 'a drawing out', a drawing out of potential already inherent in the pupil. Though as a matter of fact etymologically this definition represents a confusion between two rather different Latin roots (*educare* and *educere*), the educational point behind what is being said seems to me none the less fundamentally correct. Sometimes at the end of a seminar students will complain to me that I still haven't told them the answer, to which I always respond by challenging them to think what education is really all about. It would be very easy for the teacher with his greatly superior knowledge to engineer that the student simply follows certain well-worn tracks, and so inevitably reaches the same conclusion as him- or herself. Much more difficult, but better, is that students should first be equipped with all the resources and methodology of the teacher so that they can come in due course to informed decisions of their own. It can be a risky strategy. The student may not be willing to make the necessary intellectual effort, or there may be lots of false starts on the way. Yet even when there are false starts, more often than not the good

7

teacher is still pleased: for it demonstrates a real engagement with the issues on the part of the student. The student is no longer merely reflecting another's light. His potential is being drawn out, as he struggles towards making the knowledge his own. Then, when that finally happens, one can truly say that he possesses the knowledge in a much deeper and more fundamental way than the student who has merely learnt it from his teacher by rote.

Now let me change the analogy to one familiar to still more of you: that of parenthood. When the baby first emerges from the womb, it perceives the entire world as focused upon itself. As those familiar with the early-morning howls know all too well, parents seem to be viewed initially to be there merely to feed and to comfort, available at the baby's every beck and call. However, by about the age of two the child begins to have some notion of its own self-consciousness as something distinct from the beings and objects about it, and from then on begins the process of parental encouragement that gradually weans the child towards assigning independent value to things other than just itself. Initially, the inducement offered is more often than not merely a prudential one – reward and punishment, however subtly presented – but the hope is that this will eventually give place to properly moral considerations, sympathy and love. But to get the child there, as every parent knows, a subtle balancing act has to be played between setting boundary conditions and yet also allowing the child sufficient space to experiment and learn for him- or herself. Boundary conditions are what gives the child reassurance: that there are perceived limits, that the world is a manageable one. But space too is required, because if the child is to learn how to take responsibility for itself, it will also need the power and freedom to check out the reliability of parental claims.

These two analogies have been given because both would seem to offer excellent parallels for understanding how the Bible can be at once both that appealing and alienating mix of truth and falsehood which it discloses to us. Certainly the Bible does not hesitate to describe God as both teacher and parent. In Galatians

3, for instance, the Old Testament law is spoken of as 'our school-master to bring us unto Christ' (3.24 AV), while in Hosea 11 we have the moving description of God as parent of Israel: 'It was I who taught Ephraim [that is, Israel] to walk, I took them up, in my arms . . . I led them with cords of compassion, with the bands of love . . . and I bent down to them and fed them' (11.3–4 RSV). Whenever that passage is read, I always recall my own childhood, with its inevitable mix of boundaries and restraint which those cords or reins represent. My parents held me within a reassuring framework – those reins – as I learnt to walk, but they also gave me the freedom that made such learning possible, as I stumbled and fell, but got up again, confident in the reassurance that nothing terrible could go wrong because Mum and Dad still held me firmly within them.

So likewise, then, with God. Consider that extraordinary book, Jonah. It is in no sense history, but a profound parable of the way in which God relates to humankind. Jonah the prophet behaves like the spoilt child, but God gives him the space to learn the error of his ways. He tells him to preach repentance to the pagan city of Nineveh, but so remote are its inhabitants from Jonah's concerns that he flees, only to be trapped by God in the body of a whale. Then, having learnt his lesson – that God's care knows no bounds – once more we find him rebelling, this time when Nineveh (horror of horrors) actually repents in response to his preaching! Jonah wants to be proved right, to have his prophecies of the city's destruction fulfilled, but God has different plans, and it is only gradually that the sulking Jonah accepts the wisdom of the divine plan, as he witnesses God's concern even for the gourd that shelters him from the heat of the noonday sun.

In other words, the biblical revelation might have been very different. It might have been like a thunderbolt from the heavens; it might have been like the teacher who brooks no dissent from his own view; it might have been like the parent who stifles the child and makes him incapable of thinking for himself. But in actual fact, the reality is quite different. God valued something more highly than the immediate perception of the truth: that the community of faith should accept it for themselves, so that student could in turn become teacher, the child itself a parent.

Of the numerous examples which one might have taken to illustrate such growth of understanding within the Scriptures, let me select just one: attitudes to other nations. The history of the community of faith began like the child in the womb. For the earliest strands of the Bible indicate almost no awareness of God's concern stretching beyond the bounds of Israel. Indeed, we even have recorded in 2 Kings 5 the extraordinary story of Namaan the leper, who takes back to his native Syria a barrowload of earth because only that way is it thought that his prayers will have any prospect of being heard on foreign ground: he must stand on Jewish soil as he prays if the God of the land of Israel is to hear him. But gradually, particularly as the leaders of the nation were carted off into exile, a different lesson came to be learnt. It is very movingly expressed by Jeremiah in his letter to the captives in Babylon: 'Seek the peace of the city whither I have caused you to be carried away captives, and pray unto the Lord for it: for in the peace thereof shall ye have peace' (29.7 AV).

And so with that background firmly established, Jesus can carry this insight one stage further. Admittedly, even after Jeremiah the vision was still of other races being subject to the Jews. In chapters 60—62 of Isaiah, for instance, there is a marvellous description of the whole world streaming into Jerusalem to receive blessings. But at the same time the vision is clouded by the rest of the world being made subservient to Israel, required to bring tribute and assigned all the menial tasks. To this conception, Jesus gives an emphatic 'No'. All shall share equally in God's banquet table, as the Gentiles stream in from east and west, and from north and south, with those who think themselves first (the arrogant among his fellow Jews) last and the last first. 'From east and west people will come, from north and south, for the feast in the kingdom of God. Yes, and some who are now last will be first, and some who are first will be last' (Luke 13.29–30 NEB). The self-centred bambino has at last become the fully responsible adult.

God's care, then, is like a parent's for a child, like a teacher's for a pupil: concerned to advance understanding at their pace, not ours, so that the knowledge can truly become their own possession. But such a way of proceeding has its price. The child stumbles; the pupil misunderstands or rebels; the Bible lapses into all too human aspirations, with our own limited desires projected onto God as if they were his own. But it also has its glories. The child in due course becomes a parent, the pupil a teacher in its turn, and the community of faith one that has learnt from its mistakes, and is now ready to venture in trust into paths yet unknown, into a yet deeper understanding of the divine will and truth.

3 ✤ Conflict
in the Mines

—

Men . . . search out . . . the ore in gloom and deep darkness . . .
and the thing that is hid he brings forth to light

(Job 28.3, 11 RSV)

Chapter 28 of Job is the only passage in the Bible that alludes to
what has been the predominant experience of the great mass of
people in County Durham over the past few centuries: mining.
And what a history of conflict it has been: conflict in which the
Church has played no little part on both sides, whether one thinks
of the major role of the Methodists in securing better conditions
for the workers from their largely Anglican employers, or in this
century of the prolonged strike of the twenties in which the then
Dean of Durham, J. E. C. Welldon, only narrowly escaped being
thrown in the river at a Miners' Gala because of hostility to the
then bishop, Hensley Henson! Henson had unequivocally condemned the miners' strike, a position that was to be dramatically
reversed with regard to another strike half a century later in David
Jenkins' enthronement sermon, though even at the time some
churchmen such as William Temple, the future Archbishop of
Canterbury, showed much sympathy for the miners.

As a Christian recounting that history, there is an insidious
danger of telling it all with an artifical sense of unease – as though
as Christians we are necessarily committed to an absence of conflict, a gospel of reconciliation at any price. But the truth appears
to be that miners would have been compelled for ever to live and
work in appalling conditions, had not the weapon of the strike
been used and Christian opposed Christian. Of course we all want

a secure world, and change and conflict inevitably disturb and disorientate; but whether we look to the history of mining or to the history of God's dialogue with humanity, it would seem to me that we have no option but to acknowledge that conflict plays a key role in enlarging our perceptions and thus securing progress.

Of course, many forms of religious conflict in the past have been unqualifiedly nasty, and I am certainly not advocating a return to the era of religious wars and so forth. But the other extreme is the failure to confront our underlying disagreements, and so the Christian gospel ends up either being reduced to the lowest common denominator upon which we can all agree, or being contained within what are regarded as manageable but essentially trivial points of dissension – in much the same way as our politicians now argue over the minutiae of who will impose higher taxes rather than face the deeper, more problematic issues that confront the future of our society.

One reason why the Christian fails to see a legitimate place for conflict is of course because the Bible comes to us, as it were, already made – as a package, so to speak. Bound together as a single volume, must it not always speak as a single voice? Yet even a superficial reading of the New Testament shows that there are some conflicts to be observed; and, interestingly, in the two most obvious cases the conflict occurs between persons who already share much in common – Jesus with the Pharisees, and Paul with Peter. Then when we dig under the surface, plenty more conflict emerges: James's and Paul's very different emphases on the relative place of works and grace; or the Book of Revelation's attack on Rome as the whore of Babylon sitting uneasily with Paul's endorsement of that same authority in Romans 13; or Matthew's and Paul's charismatic understanding of structures of ministry as opposed to the more hierarchical concept which we are offered in the so-called catholic epistles of Peter and John. Nor would it be difficult to multiply these examples.

The New Testament is thus emphatically not a monolith. Rather, what we see is individuals and communities struggling to apply God's will in a constantly changing set of social circumstances, and no doubt frequently strongly disagreeing in the process, which is of course why we continue to have disagreement to this day. To give but one example, churches with a strong local congregational or charismatic basis continue to find justification in Paul, whereas those that are centrally organized with bishops can rightly observe that already according to the perspective of the later epistles of the New Testament it was thought appropriate that this earlier pattern of church government should be abandoned as divisive and fissiparous in the large institution that the Church had now become.

The period of written documentation for the Old Testament is more than ten times the length of that for the New. So, not surprisingly perhaps, there are still more conflicts to be seen just beneath its surface. For instance, Ezekiel's unqualified stress on personal responsibility ('The soul that sins, it shall die' – 18.20 AV) is undoubtedly intended as an attack on the more corporatist understandings found elsewhere, such as in the threat issued as part of the Second Commandment ('visit the sins of the fathers upon the children' – Exod. 20. 5 BCP) or the way in which a whole family is punished for a crime of which the father alone is guilty (Achan in Joshua 7). But probably the most obvious tension under the old covenant is between its three streams of prophet, priest, and wise man. Each generated its own characteristic literature and emphases: the prophet with his inspired summons to immediate social action; the priest with his stress on cult and law; and the wise man with his consideration of the ways of God as disclosed through the created order. Though they sometimes naturally flow together, as in the prophet Ezekiel's priestly concern for Sabbath and Temple (e.g. chapter 46), or the author of Ecclesiasticus' identification of the law and wisdom tradition (esp. chapter 24), no one could doubt the presence of tensions when they hear unequivocal prophetic condemnations of the sacrificial system (e.g. Isa. 1.11; Amos 5.25; Hos. 6.6), or observe the failure of most of the Wisdom literature even to mention prophet or priest.

If, then, the two-thousand-year period of biblical history is characterized by dissension, it should occasion us no surprise that such dissension has continued to occur over the next two thousand years. Once again, I must emphasize that it is not my intention to defend all the many, terrible things which have been done in the name of religion. My objective is a much narrower one than that – to.entice you away from the common, simplistic assumption that all conflict is bad, rather than what it often really is: not only creative, but *essential* as a means towards any deeper grasp of the truth. Thus it was precisely because Christians disagreed about the status and nature of Christ that the early post-biblical Church was forced to a deeper understanding of his divinity (eventually summarized in the two historic creeds) than we can find declared quite so explicitly anywhere in the New Testament. Or again, although the break-up of the Church at the Reformation was to my mind a tragedy, it undoubtedly had its compensating advantages, with its two opposed perspectives each acting as a standing challenge and reprimand to the other to rethink its ideology. Thus, dare one ask, would the missionary instinct have been quite so strong without the competitive comparison between the different denominations? Or, more fundamentally, what of the Eucharist? The Reformation rightly protested against the medieval pattern of only communicating once a year as a travesty of the New Testament norm, but in its place came another travesty: its celebration a mere three or four times a year. In theory, reading the Bible ought to have compelled an alternative pattern, but, judging by the Church of England, in the end what seems to have proved more decisive was the standing reprimand of Rome's continued weekly celebration. Or again, consider the rediscovery of the Bible which has taken place among Roman Catholics this century, and more particularly since the Second Vatican Council. What a contrast to their sixteenth-century ancestors in the north of England who during the Pilgrimage of Grace and Rising of the North did not hesitate to tear up any English Bibles they found within the cathedral church at Durham! In effecting such a change, one important element must have been the way in which Protestant engagement with the Bible over the intervening centuries constituted a constant irritant to any Roman claim to be in a real continuity with that first biblical community under Peter.

So, whether we take the Bible or the history of the Church, it does seem to me that conflict should not be derided as a wholly bad thing: it is one of the ways in which truth finally emerges. And so, equally today, we should not be unduly alarmed about disagreements within the Church; it is something that has always been, and will always be, a feature of our common search for God's message to us in our own day.

Where the problem comes is not in the conflict itself, but in how we handle it. Too often, whether out of arrogance or insecurity, we lash out, instead of humbly acknowledging that truth can come in all shapes and forms, not just from ourselves or from those with whom we have most in common. Indeed, here the Bible is surely wiser than many a modern Christian. For, despite the severity with which in its pages the surrounding religions are condemned, some of its authors did not hesitate to borrow even from them, wherever they detected the hand of God. Thus, for instance, we now know that Proverbs 22.17–23, constitutes a fairly close copy of a much older Egyptian document, *The Teachings of Amenemopet.* Indeed, this may well also be true of Job 28 itself, since it is a self-contained poem which bears no obvious relation to the rest of the book, and describes a human activity – mining – unknown to the land of Palestine.

So when we think of scholars mining deep beneath the surface of the biblical text, let us not be afraid of the apparent darkness that they may sometimes seem to engender. For out of all that darkness and uncertainty will undoubtedly come many precious gems, now brought to light. Not the least of these must surely be the realization that God works even through our conflicts and disagreements, to advance our understanding of him. For, as with Israel of old, it is by listening to those with whom we disagree that both we and they will learn.

4 ✣ The Price
Fit Only for a Slave

—

And they paid him thirty pieces of silver
(Matt. 26.15 RSV)

Peter's sermon in Acts 3 is typical of the confidence of the early Church that in Christ the Old Testament had been fulfilled. It is the same 'God of Abraham, Isaac and Jacob' (v. 13) who foretold by the prophets (v. 17) that Jesus would suffer and be raised again. Indeed, even as early as Moses God spoke to his chosen of the Christ who was to come; and, as evidence of this, Peter is portrayed as appealing to Deuteronomy 18.15: 'The Lord your God will raise up for you a prophet like me from among you' (RSV).

Such confidence of an easy match between Old Testament and New is characteristic of New Testament writing in general. However, as our understanding of the Old Testament has advanced, so has our confidence in that easy match diminished. Biblical scholars repeatedly warn us that the original point and meaning of the Old Testament passages was very different from that given to them by the apostles. Those who are aware of this phenomenon often find it rather worrying. But, far from that being the case, to me it provides a welcome release. For at last it enables us to envisage a God who treats our humanity with the utmost seriousness. However, before explaining why that is so, let me first sketch the character of the problem.

In essence, it is that, so convinced were the disciples that what happened in Jesus was a continuation of the work of the same God who manifested himself in the old covenant that they simply

17

ransacked Scripture – without reference to context – to demonstrate that this was so. Everything about the Old Testament was seen as pointing to the New, and if a verse in the Old had roughly the same form as something that had happened in Jesus' life, that was deemed sufficient to justify taking it as a prophecy of what had come to pass in his case.

The most extraordinary illustration of this is Matthew's Gospel. Repeatedly we have expressions like the following: 'All this took place to fulfil what the Lord had spoken by the prophet'. The quotation that then follows sounds apposite, but as soon as you look up the original context, problems often immediately arise. For instance, of Judas betraying Jesus for thirty pieces of silver, Matthew writes at 27.9: 'Then was fulfilled what had been spoken by the prophet Jeremiah, saying, "And they took the thirty pieces of silver . . . and they gave them for the potter's field"' (RSV). Yet only the reference to a potter's field is 'in' Jeremiah, while the thirty pieces of silver is spoken of by another prophet, Zechariah; and, more importantly, in the original context neither is thinking of the future Christ. In Jeremiah's case (32.6–15; cf. 18.2), the point of the prophet being told by God to buy the field was to reassure his compatriots that despite the external military threat, God would not abandon them, while in Zechariah 11 thirty shekels of silver is used as an image of how little the prophet's fellow nationals value a promising leader of the time. Likewise, almost every Jew contemporary with Peter would have been horrified by his interpretation of Deuteronomy. For Moses promises another prophet like himself, and that was taken to mean another great military leader who would restore the fortunes of the nation. Moreover, almost certainly that was what the passage meant in its original context.

So what then are we to do about this conflict? Most obviously, what we must not do is blame Matthew and Luke (as the author of Acts) for deliberately distorting the truth. Checking references was not as easy a matter as it is for us today. Scrolls could be quite cumbersome things to use, and indeed it seems to have been the need easily and frequently to refer to the Christian Scriptures that generated in the second century a new form of recording texts called the codex, which is the ancestor of what we would today recognize as a book. Matthew's memory clearly on occasion failed him. Was he too confident or too lazy to check, or was the scroll not easily to hand? We do not know.

More importantly, we also need to be aware that at the time neither Jew nor Christian would have read the Old Testament with any great sense of historical context. What mattered was its immediate relevance to issues of the day, and, to secure that, Jew no less than Christian can be found creating what to our mind are extraordinary readings of what was meant. A conspicuous illustration of this is afforded by what are known as Targums, contemporary Jewish explanatory expansions of the meaning of the biblical text. Take for instance 'the tree of life', to which allusion is made in the story of the Garden of Eden (Gen. 2.9). The story is all about the loss of eternal life, and until late in Jewish history any such hope was to remain absent from all their expectations. None the less, the relevant Targum comments: 'The Law is a Tree of Life for whoever strives toward it and observes its commandments: he lives and subsists like the Tree of Life in the world to come.'

This does not mean that Jews simply projected on to the Hebrew Scriptures what they already wanted to believe. The control was the desire to produce an integrated, mutually reinforcing reading of the various texts as a whole. It was precisely upon such an integrated reading that Matthew was also engaged, but significantly with one added text – the life of Christ himself. We in our own world, with its stronger sense of historical context, would do matters rather differently, but would our intention, our conviction, not be essentially the same: that whatever wrong turnings there may have been in the history of Israel, God was preparing for the day when he could send his own Son as the perfect expression of his plans for the world? The prophet or Messiah who arrived was very different from the expectations of Deuteronomy and Zechariah, but he was still the expected one, closest certainly to the teaching and experience of Jeremiah, but also with a life steeped in the Old Testament Law (of which Deuteronomy is a part) and in the prophetic witness (to which Zechariah contributes).

How this might be so demands a vast canvas, too vast to paint in any detail here. All I can do is allude to the way in which Jesus, on the one hand, intensifies and deepens the requirements of the Law, rather than abrogates it, just as on the other, he ensures that the prophetic concern for social justice shines through his teaching again and again. One has only to re-read the Sermon on the Mount to be convinced of the truth of both assertions. Ironically, we owe this also to Matthew (chapters 5—7). So, if by modern standards we must judge Matthew's use of the Old Testament as wooden in the extreme, none the less he perhaps saw more clearly than any other evangelist the proper foundations for just such a claim to essential continuity with the Old Testament witness.

But why did God not protect us from such complexities? Let us return one last time to those thirty pieces of silver. In the Law (Exod. 21.32) thirty shekels is the sum identified as appropriate compensation for accidentally killing a slave. What in the Law was a literal injunction is then taken up as a powerful image in the prophet Zechariah. Unfortunately, the original context of Zechariah 11 is now lost, but of three potential leaders ('shepherds'), a faithless people is seen as dismissing the most promising for a mere thirty shekels: 'And they weighed out as my wages thirty shekels of silver. Then the Lord said to me, "Cast it into the treasury" – the lordly price at which I was paid off by them' (Zech. 11.12-13 RSV). Talk of a 'lordly price' (RSV) or 'princely sum' (JB) is clearly sarcastic.

Whether Matthew detected the sarcasm we do not know. Certainly, if he did, it is not the focus of his concern. What matters for him is that we see Jesus as the fulfilment of Old Testament expectations, and in pursuit of that end it is sometimes suggested by New Testament scholars that he deduced the thirty pieces of silver from the Zechariah passage. The fact that only he of all the evangelists records a specific sum increases the likelihood that this was so. In any case, it was presumably difficult to discover what amount was involved, with the traitor already dead soon after the Lord whom he had betrayed.

But, as already noted, to worry about such details is to miss the basic thrust of what is being asserted: that Jesus is the culmination and perfect expression of the God already disclosed in the Old Testament. So, let me end with that very image of a price fit only for a slave. Zechariah, of course, thought that no messianic figure could possibly be valued that low, but now, as we read the Old Testament in the light of the New, that is precisely what we discover. In the incarnation God 'emptied himself, taking the form of a servant' (Phil. 2.7 RSV), thus exposing himself to all the buffeting that was the slave's lot, including crucifixion itself. But we must not confine that image of God as slave to the life of Jesus. For it was also with the weak and marginalized that he identified in that central Old Testament event of the Exodus, bringing the Israelite slaves to freedom. Not only that, he allowed himself to be buffeted again and again throughout Israel's history by a rebellious people who frequently misunderstood him, wanting to be Egyptian tyrants in their turn. Yet God's only response was the response of the weakness of the slave – not honouring power, but continuing to love even as their fortunes declined. Paradoxically, however, precisely because of that love it was this same people, the Jews, who were able to preserve sufficient of the vision for the continuity in due course to be seen.

So the question for us today is whether we too once more long to distort the vision into new forms of self-assertion, or whether we have at last learnt to accept a God who values himself precisely at this – the worth of a slave, expending himself for the weak, the despised, and the marginalized. Dare we do less?

✤ Part Two ✤
Gospel Anticipations

5 ✤ The Snake
Who Gives New Life

—

Of course you will not die. God knows that as soon as you eat it,
your eyes will be opened and you will be like gods

(Gen. 3.4–5 NEB)

I would like to end this meditation by talking about the snake that
gives new life. But let me begin with a simpler theme – Coca-Cola.
It has frequently been observed of teenagers in the Third World
that the little money they have is quite as likely to be spent on
buying a Coke as on procuring a decent meal. Why? What has
gone wrong? The explanation is not hard to find. What has happened is that the teenagers have become so duped by the adverts
that the drink has for them come to be synonymous with youth,
vitality, prosperity, and sexual attractiveness. The image has
ceased to be a pointer; it has become the thing itself. To quote the
jingle: 'Coke is the real thing'.

But before one starts to become patronizingly superior, it is
salutary to remind ourselves that exactly the same thing has happened continually in the history of Christianity. Again and again,
symbols have been taken literally, and thereby either given the
wrong kind of power or robbed of significance altogether. Probably of nowhere is this more true than of the story of the Fall.
Augustine took the story literally, and thus burdened Christianity
for more than a thousand years with the absurd belief that sexual
intercourse is necessarily impure, and consequently through it
there is passed on from generation to generation the taint of
original sin. Nowadays, our problem is rather different. We know
not to read it as fact, but because we do not seriously engage with

the symbols, the literalism is still there: the forbidden fruit remains for us just that – a piece of fruit, the fig leaves a primitive forming of clothing, and so on. So let us start again and see what we can discover.

In Romans 7 Paul puts more prosaically precisely the same point as lies behind Genesis 3: 'It was the Law that made me know what sin is. If the Law had not said, "Do not desire what belongs to someone else", I would not have known such a desire. But by means of that commandment sin found its chance to stir up all kinds of selfish desires in me . . . and it deceived me and killed me' (7.7–11 TEV). 'Adam' is in fact the Hebrew for 'man', and so the Genesis story is intended as the story of each one of us, and what is being symbolized in the eating of the forbidden tree of good and evil is that strange perversity to which Paul refers that is so characteristic of human nature: the way in which the forbidden seems to exercise a particularly compelling attractiveness for all of us. It is almost as though we are determined, whatever the cost, to prove ourselves our own master or mistress, whether it be a relatively trivial act like breaking school rules or more serious, as with experimentation with drugs or whatever. We are determined to show our independence, whereas what happens (according to both Paul and Genesis) when we try to do this is in fact a still greater dependence.

Paul speaks of us being made subject to death, but one has to turn to Genesis to discover what the nature of the connection might be. It too speaks of the loss of immortality, the loss of the tree of life, but as well it points to a deeper explanation of that than mere divine fiat. It does this through its use of the symbol of the couple's nakedness. Here the intention was never to suggest that sex from now on started to feel dirty. Nor is it just a matter of a loss of innocence. Rather, the primary reference lies in the implied loss of self-control. For a man conceals his nakedness precisely because he wants to hide what he cannot fully control, and so what the symbol underlines is that, so far from Adam and Eve gaining greater freedom by their rebellion, what in fact has happened is a deeper servitude. By choosing to make their own decisions about good and evil – by eating from the tree – they have fallen prey to a far more oppressive control than any that obedience to God could have brought. They become trapped in themselves – symbolized by the lack of control in sexual desire – whereas, had they continued to pursue the divine plan for them, they could have enjoyed real liberty.

To put the imagery in modern terms, the author is suggesting that the death of the heroin addict is the ultimate penalty towards which all human sin points. We think that the first fix, the first act of rebellion against God, will bring true freedom, whereas in fact all we are doing is setting ourselves on an inevitable path towards ultimate mortality, a state in which we will flee from allowing others to see ourselves as we are: flee from allowing our naked-ness into the full light of day.

And the solution? At last I come to the serpent with which I began. So used are we to thinking of the snake as a tempter, as the devil, that we forget that in the ancient world it was a symbol of new life, of restored health, and used as such in pagan temples whether one thinks of the Greek god Aesculapius or the Ca-naanite Eshmun. Nor is it hard to understand why. A snake can discard its old dead skin, and acquire a new one; so the thought ran, the doctor can help the patient to shed his old diseased skin, and put a new, healthy one in its place. So likewise in this case, in Genesis, the serpent is made to promise new life, immortality: 'You will be like gods'.

But the reality was very different; instead the serpent is con-demned to crawl upon the ground, made subservient, dependent like those whom he has tempted. In using the symbol thus, in all probability the author was here engaging in some hostile polemic against the established, more positive, pagan use. But that should not blind us to the fact that later in the biblical canon the symbol is once more restored to its full original meaning. Consider John 3.14: 'As Moses lifted up the serpent in the wilderness, so must the Son of Man be lifted up, that whoever believes in him might have eternal life' (RSV). The allusion is to an incident in Numbers 21, where in response to a plague of poisonous serpents Moses is advised by God to set up a bronze serpent on a standard, with the promise that whoever is bitten and looks at it will live. Whatever lies behind the original incident, St John powerfully transforms the allusion to underline Jesus' role as the new Adam, the new humanity. No more do we have a snake that crawls upon the ground, debased, dependent humanity, but a raised, uplifted serpent; lifted, admittedly, on to a cross, a dead tree, but one that can still become the tree of life precisely because it exhibits Jesus' total identity with his Father's will, his total commitment to a life for others. The old human skin, the skin of rebellious self-centredness, has been shed, and in its place has come a new skin, a skin that can bring freedom, health, and eternal life. So the choice is ours. Try to be wholly our own master and we will end up like the snake of Genesis – slimily slithering along the ground. Or live like Jesus in conscious dependence on our heavenly Father, and then we will discover that strangest of paradoxes: how taking of the fruit from a dead tree, the cross, can bring a new skin, new life, eternal life.

6 ✣ A Body
That Stretches to Heaven

—

[Jacob] dreamed that there was a ladder set up on the earth, and
the top of it reached to heaven; and behold, the angels of God
were ascending and descending on it
(Gen. 28.12 RSV)

When we pray to our Father in heaven, I'm sure that none of us
think of God as literally 'up there'. The sky is a symbol for the
other, non-material world in which our God dwells, a good symbol
wisely chosen because it emphasizes the height, the awe, the majesty, and the transcendence of God. Equally, though, if we are to
have anything to do with God, that height, that distance, has some-
how to be bridged. Primitive religions thought of mountains, trees,
and standing stones as symbolic of the gap already partially bridged
(they already point upwards), and so such spots quickly came to be
regarded as sacred. One finds such places within the Bible itself.
Thus Mamre (Gen. 13.18; 18.4) and Shechem (Gen. 12.6; 35.4)
seem to have been treated as holy places because of a tall oak or
terebinth tree growing there, while the story of Jacob's ladder in
Genesis 28 is partly told to explain the origin of a standing stone at
Bethel, since the incident ends with Jacob in verse 22 setting up as
a 'pillar' the stone that had been his pillow.

Such standing stones were the tribute of simple, uncultured
peoples to the desire for such a link between heaven and earth,
between God and humanity, and one finds them throughout the
world. A more complex form of the same symbolism that came to
be developed among the early city-dwellers of Mesopotamia was the
so-called ziggurat, a stepped platform of dressed stone that

stretched towards the heavens; the one at Babylon was over two hundred feet high. The Hebrew for Babylon is Babel, and it is thus this ziggurat which is satirized in Genesis 11 as the Tower of Babel. In that story it is clearly seen as symptomatic of human arrogance, of vain attempts to storm the heavens, and so reach God. But there seems little doubt that at least once elsewhere in the Bible the same symbol is given positive significance. For almost certainly in the story of Jacob's dream at Bethel, 'staircase' rather than 'ladder' is a more accurate translation – especially as in any case it would be hard to envisage a gainly procession of angels ascending and descending on something as small and flimsy as a ladder!

The angels upon the 'ladder' are no less symbols, though it should be noted that this is not to deny the existence of such beings. For just as I opened by saying that heaven is a symbol that points beyond to another reality, another world, so is the same true of angels. Their wings are symbols of flight, and thus of communication between heaven and earth, but in themselves they no more have wings than heaven has physical place within our own universe. Yet they must surely exist. To think of heaven as unpopulated until human beings came along would seem excessively anthropocentric. And can we really suppose that God created no form of life more like his own non-material existence than our own? In other words, like heaven above, are not angels both symbols and reality?

In Jewish thinking, in fact angels came increasingly to be used as the pre-eminent symbol for God's relation with humanity, and so where an earlier writer might have attributed an action directly to God, now it is spoken of as the action of an angel. Indeed, in parts of Scripture within a few verses the same being will now be called an angel, now God (e.g. Gen. 16.7, 13; Exod. 3.2, 4). So we should not worry overmuch whether angels were involved in specific cases or not. The underlying intention is clear: it is to say that here heaven has met earth in whatever form.

And that, of course, is the real import of Jacob's dream. Despite the trick he played on his father, Isaac, to rob his brother Esau of his inheritance, through his dream he is now promised a special relation with God, one in which all the families of the earth are to be blessed. So Jacob gives God an oath of allegiance, and sets up the pillar we have already mentioned at the renamed Bethel ('house of God') as a sign of the contact which had been established there between him and his Maker. This is not the end of the story, though. For once more in chapter 32 of Genesis we find Jacob involved in a strange experience: this time he is wrestling with a being who at times seems an angel, at others, God himself. The result is that Jacob's thigh is put out of joint, and he is given a new name, Israel, the name of the nation that is to be. We also discover a morally transformed individual. For whereas, even after Bethel Jacob was prepared to engage in deceit, cheating his father-in-law, Laban of his flocks, now he unequivocally condemns his sons, Simeon and Levi, for comparable behaviour (Gen. 34 and 49.5–7). The limping thigh is perhaps meant to tell us that he has finally learnt moral restraint.

It is only in the context of this complex web of symbolism that it becomes possible fully to comprehend the incident that concludes the first chapter of John's Gospel. Already at verse 47 we are warned of something special in the offing. For whereas Jacob had been described as approaching his brother Esau 'with guile' (Gen. 27.35), Jesus declares of Nathaniel: 'Behold, an Israelite indeed, in whom is no guile!' (John 1.47 RSV). In effect, this new 'Israel' has been declared better than the old. But yet more is to come. Jesus had seen Nathaniel sitting under the fig tree, the traditional site according to Micah of messianic expectation: 'in the latter days . . . they shall sit every man under his vine and under his fig tree, and none shall make them afraid' (4.1,4 RSV). But something greater than Jacob, greater even than the Messiah, is here. For observe how Jacob's vision is now transformed. Nathaniel is promised: 'Truly, truly, I say to you, you will see heaven opened, and the angels of God ascending and descending upon the Son of Man' (John 1.51 RSV).

Jesus has himself become the ladder, the staircase upon which angels flit to and fro from heaven. Visually, it is all rather difficult

– trying to think of some vast human figure linking heaven and earth through his body. But of course it is after all only a symbol, and significantly the promise is never literally fulfilled in John's Gospel, or for that matter in any of the other Gospels. Its real point lies elsewhere: not to tell us about angels or the size of Christ's body, but what he can now achieve for us. He is the sacred tree, the sacred pillar, the ziggurat, the ladder that can join heaven and earth, enabling us to become one with God. And we do that by identifying with his life, death, and resurrection, all of which focused upon a tree, the cross that at once pointed vertically to heaven, to God as the source of all good, and horizontally opened its arms to embrace all humankind in its love.

In this case, seeing the point of the symbolism means eliding the angels from any specific role: Christ is now there exclusively to occupy centre-stage. But that does not mean that they have gone entirely. For the beyond towards which Christ points is still a heaven of angels, a world in which 'angels and archangels and the whole company of heaven' join each Eucharist with us in the praise of him whose body stretches to the heavens precisely through being contracted to a tiny wafer or crumb – 'the Body of Christ' – in our hands. Here is our Jacob's ladder, of which we also can say: 'This is none other than the house of God, and this the gate of heaven' (Gen. 28.17 RSV).

7 ❖ Leaping over a Wall

By my God I can leap over a wall
(Ps. 18.29 RSV)

Most of us have a little bit set aside in the bank or building society for a 'rainy day', what we call our 'savings'. But, no matter how much we are inclined to worry about money, none of us will view those savings in precisely the same way as our parents or grand-parents did – as literally a lifeline, as what may prove the only means of keeping acute poverty (or even the workhouse) from the door. For, with the creation of the welfare state, saving has become for most of us a much more mundane matter. That col-lapse in the power of the word to say something about the nature of our condition finds an obvious parallel in what has also hap-pened to the biblical image. 'Saving' and 'salvation', instead of being matters of life or death, have become instead narrow, essen-tially 'churchy' terms – dead metaphors – or, almost as bad, nar-rowly identified with that over-enthusiastic brand of Christian who asks the uncomprehending passer-by, 'Are you saved?'

Behind that question, of course, lies important issues about sin and its proper relation to the cross. But if we are to recover the full power of what the Bible has to say to us, we need to begin at a far more elementary level, at the root of its metaphors. In the process what we shall discover is that sin (in the sense of specific wrong-doing) is only one of the many problems to which the notion of 'saving' is addressed. Indeed, it will probably come as a surprise to most people to learn how relatively few of the biblical uses of the Hebrew and Greek words for salvation are in fact explicitly connected to this notion of sin. For instance, in the New Testament over a third deal with deliverance from specific ills such as disease, devil possession, or death, while in the Old Testament not only does this type predominate, but more often than not the focus is the consequences of war, physical peril, or oppression.

That is no accident. For the Bible leaves nothing out of its sights. It is as concerned with our physical well-being as with our mental, a fact well illustrated by the Hebrew word for peace – *shalom* – which means both a sense of well-being and material prosperity. Literally, it means 'wholeness'. In our case, unlike our ancestors in the ancient world, what prevents such wholeness is more likely to be spiritual than material – worries and anxieties of various kinds. But we can still learn from the past, not least because the solution, the salvation that comes from God, remains essentially the same: a salvation that involves us looking out beyond ourselves.

Consider first the Old Testament usage. The root of the Hebrew word for salvation literally means 'to make room' or 'give space', and 'salvation' in this basic sense is well illustrated by the warrior's prayer of thanksgiving in Psalm 18 (esp. vs. 25–36). Because he was not hemmed in by his foes but able to move freely – even 'to leap over a wall' (v. 29) – his 'salvation', his 'victory', was secured. That is hardly a very religious context, but the transition to the more familiar setting was in fact quite easily made. Thus when Moses in Exodus 15 celebrates the destruction of the pursuing Egyptian chariots and the resultant deliverance of the children of Israel out of Egypt, his song that 'the Lord . . . has become my salvation' (v. 2) immediately resonates at two levels. In one sense he merely repeats the theme of the warrior of Psalm 18: the sinking Egyptian chariots allow the Israelites space to flee. But also there is the more profound level: no longer slaves, they now have the space to be themselves in the land the Lord has promised them. Oppression has been replaced by the possibility of expression.

That particular passage may well date from the events of the Exodus itself, though inevitably with orally transmitted poetry it will also have been the subject of some change over the centuries. But those changes are small compared with the transformation wrought in the general condition of the Israelites. No longer nomadic tribesmen, but settled agricultural labourers; and then no more a state at all, but, during and after the Exile, dispersed among the nations. Is it any wonder that the question of salvation had to be asked anew in these changed conditions? Nowadays, we would answer such questions by saying that, had Moses been alive here and now, then this is what he would have said. But in the ancient world there was no such convention, and so we find attributed to Moses ideas that really belong centuries later. Yet that should not worry us, because what we can learn from this is what the ability 'to leap over a wall', to have this sense of space – expression rather than oppression – might mean in very different social contexts.

Six hundred years or so after Moses, towards the end of the seventh century BC, a number of historians sharing a similar perspective set to work to write the history of Israel from the time of Moses to their own day, and the result was the books in our Bible from Deuteronomy to 2 Kings. In modern terms, the two least historical are Deuteronomy and Joshua, but, paradoxically perhaps, these are also in many ways the most valuable spiritually. Relevant here is the fact that they disclose very clearly what the authors think should be meant by salvation in their own particular historical context.

Deuteronomy is presented as though it were one long sermon from Moses, delivered just before the people enter the promised land. But, though concerns from that earlier period are to be found (for example, how to deal with the Canaanites still in the land), overwhelmingly it assumes a very different world, a stable agricultural community under the rule of a king, and indeed a monarchy which experience has already taught to be not without its problems (17.14–20). The move from powerlessness to power has clearly brought with it a lack of concern for the minority who continue to experience oppression, continue to feel hemmed in by their circumstances. The result is a repeated refrain within the book that all must share in the liberation that delivery from Egypt symbolized, particularly those who have no natural protectors (Deut. 10.18–19; 14.28; 15.18; 24.14–15).

The tack employed by this Second Law (the literal meaning of the Greek term 'Deuteronomy') is repeated appeal to 'remember that you were a slave in the land of Egypt'. The Book of Joshua tackles the matter rather differently. As we know from the New Testament (Matthew 1.21) Joshua literally means 'Saviour', and so it is fascinating to observe what this author understands by the salvation wrought by Joshua, Moses' successor in bringing the people into the promised land.

The book of the same name implies that the task was almost effortlessly achieved. But history is seldom that simple, and so what is now suggested by many Old Testament scholars is that the book is in fact an idealized portrait of how things might have gone, had Israel trusted in God, whereas the Book of Judges gives us the stark reality – internal feuding and slow progress towards a single, united state. But precisely because it records the ideal – what might have happened rather than what did – it can be used to pinpoint more accurately what was understood by salvation. Significantly, one repeated theme is the participation of the entire community – 'all Israel' (Josh. 3.1 etc.) – in the conquest, and thus the right of all to share in its fruits. Indeed, to be part of the people of Israel is seen as synonymous with having a portion in Yahweh's land (cf. Josh. 22.25). The Hebrew slaves had moved from oppression to expression, from being hemmed in to a sense of space, a sense of a land as theirs, as one in which under God they could *all* share.

That image of everyone having a share in the community, of everyone having 'space', is a recurring theme throughout the Old Testament. Think, for instance, of the prophet Micah's marvellous vision of an age of peace which sees as its prerequisite that 'they shall sit every man under his vine and under his fig tree, and none shall make them afraid' (4.1–7, esp. v. 4 RSV). In this vision, everyone has something to call his own, something to contribute to the greater good. Yet how unlike our own modern world, where so many in the Third World are deprived of even the basic necessities of life! Or think of our own so-called developed society, and how hard it is for the unemployed to make meaningful sense of themselves within a community where they play no part.

In the latest strand of material attributed to Moses (seen particularly in the Book of Leviticus) the issue was to change once more: dispossessed of the land, the community was now living as aliens in a foreign land. Salvation, freedom, space was now seen as coming through detailed observation of the Law. Today, that is perhaps the hardest conception for us to understand. But it can be made intelligible, and I would like to make the attempt on another occasion (cf. pp. 69–73). For the moment, though, I think that it is more important to pursue our reflections a little further into the New Testament.

If the root of the image in Hebrew is about giving people space in which to flourish, the root of the Greek metaphor lies in ideas of health and well-being. Thus, for example, in chapter 8 of Luke's Gospel, where there are three healing miracles – the Gerasene demoniac, the woman with a haemorrhage, and Jairus' daughter – most English translations rather coyly speak of 'healing' or 'making well', or perhaps just hint at something more with 'making whole', whereas the Greek unequivocally uses the same word as it used elsewhere to speak of salvation (vs. 35, 48, 50). It is not that physical health was ever seen as the whole of what is meant by salvation, but it does play a crucial role and, as any of us who have recovered from a serious illness well know, it can very effectively symbolize what it might mean to regain wholeness, to be saved from what threatens our well-being.

At the same time, the New Testament insists that for complete well-being more is required. What that more is is explicitly revealed a few chapters later in Luke in the story of the healing of the ten lepers (17.11–19). Only one returns to thank Jesus, and significantly it is only of this one that the narrative now uses the word that means both health and salvation. Jesus says: 'Arise and go thy way;

thy faith has made thee whole' (v. 19 AV). By escaping from self-absorption into thankfulness and trust towards God, he has achieved a deeper sense of wholeness than any of his companions.

It is a message that Luke still further reinforces later in that same chapter. Whereas earlier (at 9.24) he had already quoted in the same form as the other evangelists Jesus' enigmatic remark that he who wishes to save his life must lose it, now however, he paraphrases it as meaning: 'whoever seeks to possess for themselves their soul will lose it, whereas he who loses his soul will bring it to birth' (Luke 17.33, my translation). The preceding verse had cryptically warned: 'Remember Lot's wife'. Clearly, the point is that she turned into a pillar of salt because so preoccupied was she by her possessions that she turned round and thus lost everything, whereas had she faced ahead, had she looked beyond herself, then her salvation would have been assured. So by this paraphrase Luke is telling us that it is by losing ourselves, by ceasing to be preoccupied (or even obsessed) with ourselves, that we discover wholeness, a true security, a space that speaks of real freedom. And so that is why a little later the generosity of the repentant Zacchaeus is taken as the model of salvation. Not only does he restore fourfold what he has defrauded, he vows half of his goods to the poor. When Jesus comments that 'today salvation has come to this house' (19.9 JB), Luke intends us to think not only of a sinner's repentance, but also of the liberty that Zacchaeus has now acquired by turning out from himself towards others.

So there then is the Bible's larger version of salvation: of a saved community in which all have 'space', all a valued place, no longer oppressed but expressed; a community itself dependent upon 'saved' individuals, human beings healed from the oppression of self-absorption, the worry of self-concern, and thus turned out from themselves towards others and towards God. Just think how very different we as individuals and as a society might be, were we to heed that vision – the self-absorbed, no less than the poor and the unemployed to whom we referred the Old Testament image, all alike leaping over that wall into God's greater freedom!

8 ✣ A Vocation with a Gun

—

The trumpets were blown . . . the people raised a great shout, and
the wall fell down flat

(Josh. 6.20 RSV)

If one is browsing in a bookshop or library, one quickly knows
what category of book one is dealing with simply by looking at
shelf headings – novels, biography, chemistry, history, and so
forth. And even if one is rummaging through a random pile at a
jumble sale, there are still plenty of immediate clues – the blurb
on the back cover, for instance, or the foreword. But with the
books of the Bible it is quite different. When the Old Testament
was being written, there were none of the helpful conventions
that we have today. Instead, it falls to us, as we read, to work out
the nature of the material confronting us. A case in point would
be the story of Jonah and the whale. It might conceivably have
been history (there is nothing in the book to say that it is not), but
the more we reflect on the history of Judaism, the more probable
does it become that what we have here is a mighty good yarn,
which is at the same time concerned to make a theological point:
that despite the opposition even of those who claim to speak in
God's name – prophets like Jonah – God's concern extends far
beyond the Jews even to their enemies in distant Nineveh.

With Jonah we have a fairly straightforward case: it is in no
sense history, but (rather like Jesus' parables) a tale, a good story,
told to make a profound religious point. Sometimes, though,
matters are more complex. The story of the fall of Jericho (Josh.
5.13—6.20) provides an excellent illustration of this. Joshua was

39

certainly a historical figure, and so too was the city of Jericho –
even today you can visit the excavations that demonstrate the
ancient history of this beautiful, oasis town, a history that stretches
back well beyond the time of Joshua himself. All that might in-
cline us to believe that what we are dealing with here is actual
history, pure and simple, but there are a number of reasons for
being cautious.

Immediately after conquering Jericho, Joshua, we are told,
goes on to take the city of Ai, which is fine until one discovers
that the name means 'Ruin', for who in their right mind would
call the town in which they live 'The Ruin'? Then, even more
problematic, whereas the Book of Joshua describes the land
being effortlessly and immediately conquered in its entirety by
the invading Israelites, the book that follows, the Book of Judges,
presents a very different picture. Local charismatic leaders, the
judges of the narrative, are portrayed as struggling against a
much stronger, but disunited, local population. But could that
have been possible, if all the work of conquest had already been
achieved by Joshua?

So, slowly it dawns upon us that the two books of Joshua and
Judges are in fact trying to achieve very different purposes. Judges
tells us the way things actually were, and a rather depressing story
it makes, full of human fallibility and desperately inadequate conceptions of God, including even human sacrifice, as in the story of
Jephthah and his daughter. By contrast, the Book of Joshua tells
us how it *ought* to have been, with the invading Israelites in total
dependence upon God and what *might* then have ensued: instead
of having to wait several centuries before a proper nation state was
created, this could already have been achieved very much earlier,
if only tribal divisions had been overcome and concerted action
taken, all under the guiding hand of God. In other words, the
nearest modern equivalent to the Book of Joshua is the historical
romance, with its blend of fact and fiction – with the fiction added
sometimes purely for entertainment value, but sometimes – and
here we come nearer to the Book of Joshua – added also to make

a point, for instance, the distinctiveness of Scotland as a nation, or the corruption of the medieval Church.

What then are we to make of this story of the fall of Jericho? So far, no archaeological evidence has been unearthed of the city's destruction at the time of Joshua but, on the other hand, the incident of the harlot Rahab helping to betray the city seems a plausible incident, unlikely to have been invented. Yet to worry about details such as these is, as I have already tried to suggest, to miss the author's central point. We know that the two books of Joshua and Judges come from the same family of writers, and indeed could conceivably have been written by the same person. What our author has done is let the other judges survive as they were in history, but in this case transform Joshua into something very different: someone who can carry a lesson not only for the author's own day, but for ours as well.

How the use of noise had once brought about the defeat of the enemy we learn from an incident in the life of Gideon in Judges 7, but that purely secular story is transformed almost out of recognition in the telling of the capture of Jericho. Instead of an unexpected cacophony being used to deceive the enemy into thinking that a very large force was near at hand, the description is now in purely religious terms. Six days of silent, prayerful processions led by the priests are followed by a seventh on which the shofars are blown, the ram's horns still used to this day in the worship of orthodox Jews. The acts of war have thus become a religious act.

And that surely has still much to teach us. It is all too easy for us to hive off religion into a few, narrow, protected vocations – being a priest, nurse, or teacher. But that cannot be right. If God is God of all life, then being a soldier, being a businessman or being an accountant all fall equally under his concern. By fusing the image of soldier and priest into one, the author of the Book of Joshua challenges us to rethink the role of the secular. Why should the soldier, or businessman, not also be called to a vocation, to a task that is blessed by God, even though it may at times carry with it terrible costs either to oneself or to others?

Think of the soldiers who risk their own lives by taking food supplies into Bosnia – 'on a wing and a prayer', according to one U.N. commander – or think of the financial advisers who seek to secure reasonable profits for the Church from its investments, or property developments such as the largest shopping centre in Europe, the Metro Centre at Gateshead in the north of England. Just because the Church has made wrong decisions in the past – for example, supporting war when it ought not to have done so, or extorted money from the poor – that is no ground for retreating from clear acknowledgement that everything remains under God's hand. So whether it be priesthood, war, or business, each can be a vocation, each a task to which we are summoned by God.

In short, then, being religious, being holy, is not just about getting down on your knees to pray or being nice to everyone, it is also about where to invest one's money, and even, dare I say it, when to fire one's gun. War as potentially a holy business, as something which God requires us to do – there is the message in the fall of Jericho; soldiers legitimately portrayed as priests who also can make their own appropriate offering of something worthwhile to God. The walls of a city falling as a sacrificial offering, as something demanded by one's vocation: a startling challenge to our age, but certainly one worth taking seriously. Is the Christian's task not to ensure that cities like Berlin, Saigon, or Sarajevo survive or fall for the right reason, rather than that we stand self-righteously apart, wringing our hands in useless lament?

9 ✤ From Warrior to Shepherd Boy

—

There remains yet the youngest, but behold, he is keeping the
sheep

(1 Sam. 16.11 RSV)

Under David who ascended to the throne about 1000 BC, Israel
became a great empire. In a series of military campaigns he sub-
dued nearly all the neighbouring states. His dominions reached
as far as the Red Sea in the south, while in the north Syria had an
occupying garrison imposed upon it. Eastwards he conquered
Transjordan, while westwards he pushed to the sea, bringing the
Philistines under his control. Yet within less than a century all this
was to disappear. Only his son Solomon enjoyed comparable success, and on that monarch's death in 922 the empire disinte-
grated, never more to return (unless one were to count the
successes of the modern Israeli army).

The events which immediately precipitated that collapse are
described in 1 Kings 12. Solomon's successor, Rehoboam, is asked
to moderate the centralizing policy of his father which had resulted in large taxes, but responds: 'My father chastised you with
whips, but I will chastise you with scorpions.' The result is Jeroboam's revolt, and the permanent division of the country into two
distinct nations. So much of the Bible assumes knowledge of the
consequences of that division, that what I want to do is explore
that history and consider what it might possibly have to teach us in
our own practice of faith.

Though the southern kingdom retained Jerusalem as its capital, economically it was really the northern kingdom that was by

far the more significant of the two. One indication of this is the fact that the northern kingdom retained the name of Israel, with the southern part being known henceforth as Judah (the Judaea of Jesus' day). Much of this southern part of the country was desert, and even at its largest extent under King Josiah the capital of Jerusalem is estimated to have had a population of only 25,000. By contrast, the north was not only largely green and fertile, but also transversed by the major trade route between Egypt and Mesopotamia through the Valley of Jezreel known as the 'Via Maris' or Sea-Route. Though Judah did have one obvious psychological advantage in having within its borders the city which David had made his capital, this was compensated for in the north by strong tribal loyalties, particularly through the most powerful of these, Ephraim, the name sometimes used by the prophets to speak of Israel as a whole. But it was only really with King Omri's founding of a capital at Samaria (and note the name, from which of course comes the adjective 'Samaritan') that a strong northern identity was at last formed.

However, being on the world's trade routes also has its negative side: that very accessibility means being accessible not just for caravans of commerce, but also vehicles of war; and so despite its greater natural resources, it was the northern kingdom which first fell to a foreign occupying power, in 722 BC, with Judah surviving for another 135 years until 587. With both lands now occupied, that might have been a time for reconciliation, but instead attitudes seem to have hardened; and so when a more tolerant occupying power, the Persians, decided to allow the rebuilding of Jerusalem, the northerners at first protested – and then when they changed their minds and offered to help, this help was refused.

Other factors no doubt contributed as well, but certainly what we have by the time of Jesus is two very different identities confronting one another, Judaea in the south and Samaria further north, distinguished now not only by a different history, but also by different religious practices. Then, to complicate matters still more, even further to the north lies a third region, Galilee, which once had been purely pagan – Isaiah calls it 'the land of the Gentiles' (9.1) – but which now had a large Jewish population, settlers from the south. This was a movement that greatly accelerated in the century after Jesus' death as a result of the major revolts which took place in Judaea against the Roman occupying power.

So much, then, for our history lesson. What can it teach us about the ways of God?

For me, the most astonishing aspect is the way in which God again and again confounds human notions of greatness, and advances his purposes not through the mighty of this world, but through the insignificant. Economically, as I have already indicated, the future of the Jewish faith ought to have lain with the northern kingdom of Israel, but that was not to be. Though some of the writers of the Old Testament stem from the northern kingdom, overwhelmingly they are from the south, from Judah, and it is Judah which stamps its mark on the future direction of understandings of faith that were eventually to culminate in Christianity.

Then, though the tradition records that Jesus was born in Bethlehem, only a few miles distant from Jerusalem, it also related that his parents came from Nazareth in distant Galilee, and it is to distant Galilee that Jesus returns; it is there that he spends his youth, and there that he exercises his ministry before the final fateful journey to Jerusalem and death. Once more, this is not what one would have expected. The centre of the cultural and religious life of Judaism lay in the south, and Galilee, though now having a large Jewish population, was still ethnically very mixed. A Jew living in the south in Jerusalem would have regarded Galilee as a stale backwater, in much the same way as today's Londoner can often be found despising the north of England. Yet it was from that northern outpost that not only Christianity took its origins, but also the future shape of the Jewish religion, since it was here after the revolt against Rome that the Mishnah and

Palestinian Talmud came to be written, two works definitive for contemporary Judaism.

Jesus' teaching is full of declarations of the reversal of the world's values, of the humble being exalted and the proud laid low, of faith as tiny as a mustard seed blossoming into a large tree, and so forth. Perhaps we think that there is a certain poetic justice in it all, but in our more worldly moments – which come all too frequently – we are inclined to doubt whether this can really be so. We ask, does this ever happen? Does God really ever bring this about?

It is in response to doubts such as these that the history which I have just related comes with an unequivocal answer – not Israel, but Judah; not Judaea, but Galilee. Again and again, we have the reversal of what we would expect. Twice in the patriarchal narratives with which the Bible begins, a younger son is chosen by God in preference to the elder – Isaac, not Ishmael; Jacob, not Esau. That was but a foretaste of what was to come. Despite all its natural wealth, the Israel that was Samaria has all but vanished from the face of the earth, with only a few hundred Samaritans left, living in the vicinity of present-day Nablus. By contrast, it was Isaiah's Galilee of the Gentiles, the despised far north, that guaranteed the future of both Judaism and Christianity, and ensured that the latter faith spread throughout the world to all the nations – the Galilee of the Gentiles now in quite another sense – no more just a land of mixed race, but the land which brings good news to all races.

David, the mighty warrior and great king, began as a shepherd-boy (1 Sam. 16.11). But the future was not to lie with his victories nor with the empire that he created, but in the all-powerful God seen as humble shepherd (John 10.10–17). The wheel had thus come full circle in the new David. But what of our own lives or the present Church? Are we Israel or Judah, Judaea or Galilee, the despising superior or the despised inferior? There is something for our thoughts and prayers.

10 ✤ Reading Between the Lines

—

> Omri did what was evil in the sight of the Lord, and did more evil
> than all who were before him
> (1 Kings 16.25 RSV)

Even if you have not read about them recently, so dramatic is their presentation that readers will have little difficulty in recalling the turbulent relations which existed between the prophet Elijah and King Ahab and his Queen, Jezebel. Perhaps the most famous incident is the story of Naboth's vineyard: when Naboth refuses to sell his estate, a trumped-up charge is arranged, Naboth put to death and his land duly expropriated for the royal estate (1 Kings 21). Jezebel is portrayed as even more wicked than her husband, and so in the way the story is told there is a certain appropriateness in her death: she is thrown from a window, trampled under foot by horses, and then her corpse eaten by dogs, just as Elijah had foretold (2 Kings 9.30–37).

The author of Kings is a marvellous story-teller, and we are easily swept along by his moral and religious indignation against the conduct of the king and queen, with pagan worship allowed in Israel and dubious moral practices used to advance the power of the monarchy. As such, it is very easy to assume that this is the only possible way in which the story could have been told, especially as it is the only continuous narrative account of the reign that we possess – apart from the later Book of Chronicles, which in any case does nothing to undermine the version in Kings. None the less, modern biblical archaeology now enables a very different account to be told. But this, far from undermining the biblical version, in fact enables it to speak to us today all the more effectively. As I shall try to demonstrate, when we compare the two versions, the biblical one emerges as a powerful challenge for us to reflect today on how God views our own nation's life and history, as distinct from the way in which we might naturally be inclined to interpret it.

Let me begin then by presenting you with the secular historian's view of Ahab's family. David and Solomon reigned between about 1000 BC and 922 BC, and during this period Israel became a great empire; it encompassed not only the present occupied territories, but also much of what currently belongs to Jordan, Egypt, and Syria, indeed including even the city of Damascus itself. Although David was largely responsible for these conquests, his son Solomon consolidated the empire by producing efficient administrative structures, and also by beautifying the new capital, Jerusalem. Unfortunately, thereafter everything then began to go wrong under Solomon's son, Rehoboam, who was, to put it bluntly, a fool. The result of a revolt against the harsh measure of his rule was the creation of two kingdoms: one very much larger in the north (still called Israel) under the successful leader of the revolt (Jeroboam), and the small part of the country still remaining loyal to Rehoboam in the south (now called Judah).

They were never again to become a united, independent nation before being artificially united once more, centuries later, under an occupying power. But things might have been very different. To see how, let's jump a century. The year is 876 BC, and someone called Omri has just become King of Israel, that is to say, the northern kingdom. This time, we have no fool. What Omri would like to do is restore the glories of the Davidic empire, but he realizes he must proceed by careful stages if this is to prove possible. So he reorganizes the country internally, builds a new capital at Samaria, and secures his borders to the north and south in order to make possible military advances eastwards. He protects his flank to the south by making peace with the southern kingdom, Judah, and his flank to the north (present-day Lebanon) by marrying his son, Ahab, to the daughter of the Phoenician King of Sidon, Jezebel. That way, he can confidently advance his territories to the east, and this he does: recapturing Jordan (Edom) and defeating in battle Behadad, King of Syria. This policy is then continued under his son, Ahab, who strengthens further his southern flank by marrying his daughter Athaliah to the King of Judah, and indeed she even succeeds in becoming monarch of the southern kingdom in her own right, the only female monarch in the history of the two kingdoms. Perhaps it is little wonder, then, that archaeologists have discovered that more than a century after his death Omri was still being mentioned with respect in far-off Assyria (modern-day Iraq).

Now such consolidation and expansion was of course not achieved without a price; in particular, the religious price was greater toleration of pagan gods, with Jezebel bringing her own priests to look after her, and along with that went a moral laxity that subordinated everything to the royal interest. The result is that, whereas from a secular viewpoint Omri was seen as one of the great kings of Israel (certainly the greatest after David and Solomon), the Bible reduces him to a mere five verses; Ahab, his son, is admittedly given more space, but this is only because of Elijah's attempts to oppose him. In short, secular greatness is reduced by the Bible to mere moral turpitude.

Nor is this treatment by any means unique. A century later, we have the only other king of Israel who is of significant secular importance, Jeroboam II, who reigned for forty years (786–746 BC). This time the author of Kings does at least concede his military successes (2 Kings 14.23–29), but there remains no acknowledgement that it was a time of unparalleled prosperity for the kingdom. Instead, we are simply told that 'he did what was evil in the sight of the Lord'. It is a pattern which we find repeated in what is the oldest book in the Old Testament, the writings of the prophet Amos. Certainly, reading between the lines of the prophet's text we discover that it was a period of unparalleled building and prosperity. Houses were now increasingly of stone

(5.11), beds were made of ivory (6.4), and had damask cushions (3.12), while food was choice lamb with wine by the bowlful (6.4–6). In particular, the prosperity and luxury of the capital Samaria was a source of envy and jealousy to surrounding nations. But Amos' focus insistently remains elsewhere: not at all on Jeroboam's achievements, but on their social cost.

Prosperity had brought with it the loosening of social ties, as had the migration of population to the capital. The people of the countryside now seemed distant, a different social class rather than part of the same nation, while wealth acquired as a result of war meant that some had forgotten what it meant to be poor and its terrible consequences. The result was that exploitation of others now no longer seemed such a terrible sin. So, for example, to help pay for fine houses, heavy levies of grain were imposed upon the rural poor, and even dishonesty resorted to in the courts (5.10–12).

With a clarion call like 'let justice roll down like waters, and righteousness like an ever-flowing stream' (5.24), it would be all too easy to portray Amos' response as that of the radical egalitarian, but my suspicion is that this would be to miss the point. Amos came from the more cohesive, but less prosperous, southern kingdom of Judah, and what he and Elijah were reacting against was the way in which increasing prosperity brought with it a declining sense of social responsibility, a declining sense of what we owe to each other as opposed to what we can get for ourselves.

And do we not have there a parallel with our own society? Britain as a nation has certainly in recent years become more prosperous, with a faster growth rate than most other European countries, but with that has also often gone less compassion for the poorest elements in our community – something one finds reflected both in social attitudes and in specific political proposals (from the left as well as from the right). Indeed, however one votes, it is hard not to detect a weakening in our sense of mutual responsibility for one another.

Yet may not the problem run deeper still, with the very notion of community – the bonds that bind the better-off no less than the poor – itself now under threat? To my mind, a conspicuous manifestation of this trend lies in our now almost exclusive emphasis on rights rather than duties, and the resultant concern with how the attainment of such rights can best be measured. In itself, there is of course nothing necessarily wrong with such questions. Parents naturally want to know how far their rights for their children have been secured (how much do they know?); patients, to what they are entitled from their doctor (how long will I have to wait for an operation?). But an exclusive stress on such elements can so easily go dangerously wrong, and it seems to me not implausible to suggest that this is exactly what is happening in Britain today. Think for instance of all these recent cases of sentences being quashed because of police having tampered with the evidence in order to secure a conviction. If the police are to be judged solely by the number of successful convictions, does it not become a natural temptation to cook the books, especially if you believe someone to be guilty in any case? And what of the teacher, doctor, or priest? Does this passion for the measurable not mean that everything becomes subordinate to a concern for the best statistic: number of A levels produced rather than time 'wasted' with the less bright child; the book published in time for the academic audit rather than when fully and carefully researched; and so the list might go on. It all reaches its ultimate nadir in that terrible word 'accountability', which is simply a polite way of saying that we no longer trust one another: instead, we say, there must always be a check, a measurement on how far we are really safeguarding each others' rights.

What a contrast from a society based on a sense of duty and commitment to one another! – one in which it would simply be assumed that teachers are devoted to the education of the children committed to their charge, academics to the advancement of learning, priests to worship, mission, and pastoral care, and so on. Perhaps I'm wrong, but it does seem to me that if we had someone like Elijah or Amos in our midst, what they would see is not a society at last getting its act together, but one in the throes of a fundamental moral malaise, with such an exclusivist stress on rights, measurement and accountability all pointing to a society in the process of moral distintegration, a society in which we believe we can no longer trust one another to do our duty – in short, a society without moral backbone.

To recover what a secular historian might have made of the history of Israel, we need to do quite a lot of reading between the lines. The point, however, applies equally in the opposite direction. God's spokesmen, the prophets Elijah and Amos, saw social disintegration where their contemporaries acknowledged only advancing prosperity. Are we not today perhaps called to a similar reading between the lines?

11 ✤ Creation's Swell

—

Thou didst crush the heads of Leviathan
(Ps. 74.14 RSV)

About 620 BC a reforming movement under King Josiah attempted to centralize all worship in the Temple at Jerusalem. According to the biblical narrative (2 Kings 23), the other shrines were all essentially pagan. Yet a rather different picture emerges elsewhere, with, for instance, Jacob portrayed as founding the 'high places' at Bethel and Shechem (Gen. 28.22; 33.18–20) and Samuel seen as presiding at Ramah (1 Sam. 9.12–24). The truth seems to be that only gradually did the Jerusalem Temple assume the absolute prominence it was to have in later Judaism. That gradual growth is also reflected in the Psalter, which appears to have taken many centuries to reach its present form. We do not know how many of the psalms may once have had an independent existence, but certainly those that have survived were all to be incorporated into its worship.

So used are we to hearing psalms to the accompaniment of an organ that it comes as something of a surprise to note the range of instruments actually used in the Temple – lyre, harp, horn, trumpet, cymbals, and tambourine. In 2 Chronicles we are told that a hundred trumpeters were present at the dedication of the Temple under Solomon, not counting the other instruments. Fortunately, all this took place in the open air; otherwise, the noise might have been rather deafening! It all sounds suspiciously more like the exuberance of a Salvation Army band than the stately character of Anglican chant! However, before we jump from one

53

extreme to the other, we need to recall the extraordinary variety of material within the collection. Much of it is of a purely personal character, and so its use would of necessity have had a more intimate feel. Half the Psalter is of this character, and in fact one cannot but be impressed by the range of human experience and emotions that the psalms succeed in capturing, from joy (e.g. Ps. 30) to sorrow in all its manifest variety – from illness (e.g. Ps. 38) to despair (e.g. Ps. 88).

Among the community psalms there is a similar variety. Here we have great state occasions such as the coronation of the king (Ps. 2 and 110) or a royal wedding (Ps. 45); here, special religious occasions such as a corporate thanksgiving (Ps. 67) or a corporate lament (Ps. 80). Pilgrimage too is generously represented, essential of course for a religion which required periodic visits to the Temple in Jerusalem throughout the year. These are among the most beautiful in the Bible, the so-called Songs of Ascent (Ps. 120–134), including one of the most delightfully gentle and meditative, Psalm 131, often thought to have been written by a woman because of the images it uses.

Yet that variety is even greater than might initially have been supposed. For what we discover is Israel borrowing from pagan religion even at the heart of its own worship; and it would seem to me that this has much to teach us in respect of our own attitude to the other religions in our midst. The Jewish equivalent of our autumnal Harvest Thanksgiving was the Feast of Tabernacles, but it was altogether a richer and more exciting occasion than contemporary practice. Not only did the people take to living in tents for a short time to remind themselves of the way God had delivered their ancestors from Egypt, modern scholarship now suggests that this was also the time for a great celebration of creation within the Temple itself, a celebration which did not hesitate to borrow elements from the surrounding pagan culture.

The relevant psalms (Ps. 47, 93, 96–99), now known as the enthronement psalms, portray God as enthroned anew over the powers of chaos into which the world might otherwise dissolve were it not for his sustaining care. Powerful metaphors are used to reinforce this picture, particularly the threatening image of the waters of chaos once more about to rise up to engulf the land, but God turning them back:

> The floods have lifted up, O Lord,
> the floods have lifted up their voice,
> the floods lift up their roaring.
> [But] mightier than the thunders of many waters,
> mightier than the waves of the sea
> the Lord on high is mighty!
>
> (Ps. 93. 3–4 RSV)

Such imagery of course reflects a pre-scientific view of the world, with waters envisaged under the earth and at the world's edge, only held in check by divine decree. But that should not blind us to the profound insight contained in this powerful imagery: that creation is not just a doctrine about what happened millions of years ago, but also about what happens in the here and now; that it is only by virtue of God's sustaining power that the world is in existence at all, at this or any moment. Each year we celebrate the new life that is Easter. Have we perhaps not lost something by not also celebrating annually the miracle of creation, that the world and its beauty is also an ever-recurring divine gift, something that would disappear altogether were it not for the sustaining power of God?

But from where did Israel derive this insight? There would seem little doubt that it came through interaction with their pagan neighbours. The Babylonian Enuma Elish story had spoken of an ordered creation as the result of a battle between the gods, the god Marduk triumphing over the goddess of the disordered waters, Tiamat. At one point in the story Tiamat appears to disguise herself as a sea-monster, and it is this element which appears in the Canaanite version of the story, with Baal battling it out with Lotan, who duly appears in our Bible as the monster Leviathan. Thus both versions may well be present in Psalm 74: 'Thou didst divide the sea by thy might; thou didst break the heads of the dragons on the waters. Thou didst crush the heads of Leviathan' (Ps. 74.13–14 RSV).

The Enuma Elish myth was only discovered in Iraq in 1849, while our detailed understanding of Canaanite mythology is even more recent, this being largely due to discoveries at Ras-Shamra, the ancient Ugarit, in 1928. The Bible's principal story of creation is also affected, since there would seem little doubt that behind the 'deep' (Hebrew – 'tehom') of the second verse of the Bible lies the Babylonian goddess herself. For 'Tiamat' is etymologically related, and thus shares the same root meaning of 'sea'.

To concede this much may seem to undermine any claim to distinctiveness – not to say, uniqueness – for the biblical revelation, but this is not so. For it is one thing to admit borrowings; quite another to fail to observe their transformation. For the Bible shows no awareness of creation as a battle with another divine being as equal, far less the use of that goddess's body to create the ordered world. The divine fiat was enough to make the result unequivocally good, a fact emphatically repeated no less than six times in Genesis 1 ('And God saw that it was good'). The imagery may thus still be of battle, but it is of a battle of whose issue there is never any doubt, nor of the loving goodness with which it is waged. Compared with God, Leviathan is a mere plaything with which he may sport (Ps. 104.26); and if parts of the Old Testament still seem to treat his existence semi-literally, for Isaiah he is no more than a mere token of all that is opposed to the redemption of God's people, and for that very reason his destruction is assured (Isa. 26.20—27.13).

Yet that is not to say that Israel owed nothing more to its pagan neighbours than the power of this imagery. So far as we can gather, it was thanks to them that Israel also learnt that their God should be seen not just as a God of mighty acts of deliverance such as the Exodus, but also responsible for the ordered pattern of the world: an ordered pattern not given just once in the past, but daily sustained by the immanent purposes of God in the world that is his own.

Nor is this by any means an isolated example. Thus it seems largely under the influence of the Zoroastrian religion of their Persian conquerors that the Jews developed a more positive concept of the after-life, and with it a more developed angelology and demonology, and thus along with it, the transformation of Satan from the servant of God as he still is in the opening chapter of the Book of Job. Nor did the process cease with Christianity. Not only does one of our creeds (The 'Nicene') borrow from pagan thought ('of the same substance') in order to express better what we understand by the Trinity, even under persecution the early Christians did not hesitate to draw upon pagan mythology to illustrate what lies at the heart of Christian belief. In the Roman catacombs we find the story of Hercules and Alcestis used in one tomb on the Via Latina to characterize the resurrection: Christ, like Alcestis, died for others, and in the same way that she was summoned back from the dead by Hercules, so is he by his Father. Indeed, there is even such an example from beneath the Vatican itself, with Christ decked out with all the accoutrements of the Sun-God.

So, when you hear passages of Scripture quoted that deny the legitimacy of all contact with other religions, remember that beneath the surface lies a very different reality. Of course, the biblical community did tread with care, and so sought to maintain its distinctiveness. But that emphatically does not mean that it was above learning. The annual celebration of the swell of the waters and their abatement tell a very different story. The 'sea of glass' in the Book of Revelation (4.6; 15.2) recalls the vast bronze water basin in the Temple precinct that served as a perpetual reminder of that debt. So, if the biblical community was not above learning from other religions, why should we be?

12 ✦ Fortune's Dice

—

I bless the Lord who gives me counsel; in the night also my heart instructs me (Ps. 16.7 RSV); I will thank the lord for giving me warning; my reins also chasten me in the night season
(Prayer Book version)

Anyone accustomed to hearing the Psalter both in its Prayer Book version and in modern translations will long since have observed marked differences between them not just in language, but also in content. For instance, the man who is blessed in the Prayer Book's version of Psalm 84 because 'going through the vale of misery' he 'uses it for a well', has become in the New English Bible a prosaic traveller in a thirsty valley who has been fortunate enough to 'find water from a spring'; or again, the comforting reassurance to the dying and mourners in Psalm 23 that 'though I walk through the valley of the shadow of death, I shall fear no evil' emerges in the Jerusalem Bible as 'though I pass through a gloomy valley, I fear no harm'. In both cases, the modern version is undoubtedly a more accurate translation of the Hebrew original, but with that admission disappears also two of the most profound references to suffering in the Old Testament.

The two cases just mentioned are paralleled by similar problems in respect of Psalm 16. Take almost any modern translation, and you will discover a theme which is simplicity itself, the author's overwhelming gratitude to God for the blessings God has showered upon him: 'The lines have fallen for me in pleasant places; yea, I have a goodly heritage . . . Therefore my heart is glad, and my soul rejoices; my body also dwells secure' (vs. 6–9

RSV). That basic theme is also the primary meaning detected by major Reformation figures such as Luther and Calvin, or in England by an early translator like William Tyndale, or Miles Coverdale himself, the Puritan bishop responsible for the version we now find in the Prayer Book. Yet there is one major difference. All four thought that where the meaning of the Hebrew was in doubt, one should assign the most profound meaning possible, compatible with the direction of Scripture as a whole. The result is two significant divergences from what you will find in any modern translation. Both, like my two earlier examples, concern the question of suffering.

In verse 2 modern translations endorse the Latin version of the Bible, Jerome's Vulgate: 'I have no good apart from thee' (RSV); 'Thou, Lord art my felicity' (NEB). More than five hundred years earlier, however, Greek translators in what we call the Septuagint had offered a very different translation – that God has 'no need of our goods' – and it is this account which finds its way into the Prayer Book ('my goods are nothing unto thee'). It is also the version that finds favour with Calvin, who uses it to reinforce one of the great Reformation themes, that nothing *we* do can affect our standing with God. Prosperity or the happy life does not come because we earn it, but purely through the graciousness of God. For, as Calvin puts it, 'all the services which can yield him are in themselves things of nought, and undeserving of any recompense'.

The translation of both Septuagint and Calvin are without doubt wrong. But the sentiment is surely right, and, if anything, deepens the meaning of the psalm. Thankfulness to God cannot, and must not, be merely a disguised form of self-congratulation. Three of my school-friends are already dead, two in road accidents, the third collapsing in the street a year ago. What could be more perverse, were I to say that there was something about me which deserved to survive, and not them! No, what we thank God for is the way in which he works through our lives, giving them meaning, purpose and peace – in both good and ill.

And it is that ill which Coverdale, along with Tyndale, finds explicitly mentioned in verse 7: 'I will thank the Lord for giving me warning: my reins also chasten me in the night-season.' Once more, the translation is wrong, but ironically the fault this time is the other way round, with the Greek Septuagint right and the Latin Vulgate wrong. Thus Calvin correctly translates, as in the Revised Standard Version: 'I bless the Lord who gives me counsel; in the night also my heart instructs me.' For him, we have here a reference to night-time 'secret inspirations' and 'making progress under tuition'. But to my mind it is the wrong translation, the Vulgate, with its reference to suffering, that is the more profound.

Luther certainly thought so. For, taking his cue from the use of verse 10 in Acts (2.25 ff; 13.35) to refer to Christ's resurrection, he reads the whole psalm as a meditation on the life of Christ, with this verse as pivotal. 'The night season' is 'adversity' and the 'reins' or 'kidneys' are a reference to Christ's 'sensibility and carnal passions', the result being that, for him, the verse becomes equivalent to Hebrews 5.8: Christ 'learned obedience by the things which he suffered' (AV).

Coverdale is more concerned to apply the psalm to us all. Its superscription 'a Mictam of David' was commonly interpreted at the time of the Reformation as meaning a 'golden jewel', and significantly that is precisely how Coverdale regarded suffering. His longest work is entitled *A Spiritual and Most Precious Pearl*. In it God is portrayed as father, mother, and schoolteacher, each of whom scolds, cajoles, and punishes in order ultimately to benefit the child. For most of us, the stress is, I suspect, in the wrong place. It is not so much a case of God bringing suffering upon us, as him enabling us to use our suffering creatively, to learn trust and patience through it.

Even so, have not Luther and Coverdale alerted us to something important: that our thankfulness needs to emerge out of life's knocks as well as its pats on the back, out of our dis-ease as well as our ease? Of course we must not pretend that it is easy; and for many, such good as emerges will come despite, not because of, the pain. However, we also need to recall from time to time that at least in the affluent West we live in a world in which pain has never been less, and yet we have never complained more. Just think what the extraction of a tooth or arrow was like before today's anaesthetics, or the constant pain from the 'stone' (kidney or gall stones) that so many of the older generation would have suffered as they went about their daily business. Yet again and again we read of their refusal to be daunted. Consider, for instance, John Cosin, the principal architect of the 1662 Prayer Book. As he lies dying, he does not hesitate to throw off the bandage from his aching head, because only with hat removed, as it were, can he meet the Lord to whom he owes all; or think of Beethoven's response to the news that his deafness was incurable: he prays that 'charmed by the divine Artist he may fearlessly strive upwards'. Cannot then I, who have led such a gentle life, thank God for the public humiliations which have chastened my pride – even being lampooned in *The Times*! – or for the compassion I have learnt for others through having had the misfortune to fall in love with a married woman?

And so to my conclusion, and a strange irony. It is not impossible that the theology of the original author of Psalm 16 was not only less subtle than what came afterwards, but is even in direct contradiction. For according to some biblical scholars, in the use of the image of the cup as a sign of one's fortune (v. 5) what we have here, as in Psalm 11, is a reference to drinking as a Temple test for one's lot, as in the terrible ordeal required of the adulterous woman in Numbers 5 (vs. 23–28), where she is made to drink a strange potion to prove her innocence. If so, what the author would be celebrating would be something more like a win on the football pools, a lucky chance, rather than any deep and profound sense of intimacy with God.

But need that worry us? Luther tells us that the cup of verse 5 is a symbol for Scripture, and, as with all cups, it 'has the dregs of the letter mixed in with it'. What matters for him is the extent to which it can speak to us in the here and now of Christ, of both his cross and of the 'inheritance' of new life which that brings. And, though on this occasion Luther does not mention it, where is that image of the cup more effectively transformed save on Christ's own lips? The cup of suffering in Gethsemane (Mark 14.36) was accepted as the means for us all to drink anew of the fruit of the vine in the kingdom of God (cf. v. 25): suffering transformed into joy.

For a number of us, like the psalm's original author, the cast of the dice has fallen on a fair and lovely ground. Like some of my readers, each day as I awake I am able to thank God anew for the lovely beauty of his world, and my own good fortune within it. Yet one cannot fail to recall that dice were also being cast as Christ hung on the cross. What may prevent us from repeating the indifference of the soldiers is those inspired mistranslations from the Reformation. For, thus armed, when our own time comes, we too may be able to 'use the vale of misery for a well'. God grant that it may indeed be so.

13 ✣ God's Lunatic

—

Now as I looked at the living creatures, I saw a wheel upon the
earth . . . one for each of the four of them
(Ezek. 1.15 RSV)

Next to the Exodus, and perhaps even surpassing it in importance, the Exile was to prove a formative experience in shaping the
faith of Israel. Lost now in the mists of the distant past, the Exodus spoke of oppression only slowly yielding to freedom and
deliverance. Now that hope was to be fired again, but in the
interim the community had first to come to terms with oppression
and despair of the moment.

The prophet Ezekiel's ministry coincides with that definitive moment. Called in 593 BC, his ministry was to last until 571, a further
sixteen years after the collapse of the southern kingdom before the
invading Babylonian armies. So traumatic was the experience of
having its leading citizens carried off into exile and the land ruled by
a foreign power, that despair was perhaps the obvious reaction. No
one, though, responded more strangely than Ezekiel. He became as
it were, God's lunatic. Yet it is a lunacy that has much to tell us not
only about the nature of prophecy, but also about ourselves.

That Ezekiel was a strange character, no one could possibly deny.
Indeed, many commentators have diagnosed him to have been suffering from some form of mental illness, perhaps, schizophrenia – a
diagnosis that on first reading might seem amply confirmed by the
first few chapters of his book. Thus, in his call to the ministry,
recorded in chapter 2, he receives a scroll with the instruction to
pronounce, 'lamentations, wailings, moanings' (2.10 JB), which he

THE WORD TO SET YOU FREE

thereupon immediately *eats* and declares: 'I ate the scroll, and it tasted sweet as honey' (3.3 JB). In the following chapter he has a vision of the glory of Yahweh, as a result of which he is struck dumb, with his tongue firmly stuck to the roof of his mouth. By chapter 4 we find him lying for 390 days on his left side and then 40 days on his right, while by chapter 5 he is anticipating present-day skinheads, by shaving off first one-third of his hair, then a further third, and then the final third. And so the list could go on – all apparently justifying the view that we are confronted with some sort of lunatic.

But to leave the matter there would seem to me to offer a very shallow judgement. That is why we need to probe deeper. In so doing, we shall not eradicate the strangeness, but attention to the two factors I am about to mention will, I hope, at least make Ezekiel a more appealing figure – and also, in the process, say something important to us as well.

The first is the nature of the prophetic task. A common misconception is that prophets were primarily concerned with foretelling the future, and even today one gets silly radio and television programmes broadcast in America that claim to be able to detect contemporary events in the writings of the Hebrew prophets. Yet so far is this from being true that there are even instances in the Bible where the prophets envisaged a future scenario totally different from what in fact turned out to be the case. For example, in Jeremiah 26 we are told how the people contemplated putting Jeremiah to death because of his prophecies of immediate destruction, but decided against it when they recalled similar prophecies of the prophet Micah that had not come to pass, and which they therefore regarded not as predictive but as conditional – that is to say, conditional on how the people responded to God's demands. An even more startling instance is the prophetess Huldah. In 2 Kings 22 we find her promising King Josiah a peaceful death 'because thine heart was tender, and thou hast humbled thyself before the Lord' (v. 19 AV), but, despite him being the most devout of kings and despite this prophecy, the following chapter duly records his death on the battlefield of Megiddo (23.29).

GOD'S LUNATIC

In fact, the real thrust of the prophetic task lay in quite another direction – in *forthtelling* rather than foretelling: that is to say, in setting forth God's purposes for their contemporaries, whether it be reproach for past failures or encouragement towards a better future.

It is against this kind of background as an objective that Ezekiel's strange conduct begins to become comprehensible – strange conduct that is shared, though in a less pronounced form, by many of the other prophets. For example, one may recall the odd names Isaiah gives to his children (Chear-jashub – 'a remnant shall return', or Maher-shalal-hash-baz – 'speedy spoil, quick booty'); or Amos' use of action puns – for instance, picking up a basket of ripe fruit, the Hebrew for which is very similar to the word for destruction.

In other words, the strange conduct of these prophets is simply a dramatic way of getting a point across to a people who are otherwise reluctant to listen. One couldn't help but pay attention to Ezekiel's extraordinary actions, and, while the attention of his audience was caught, Ezekiel expounded their symbolic significance. For instance, in chapter 12 he mimes the part of a refugee suddenly driven forth from his home, by packing a few possessions, knocking a hole in the side of his house, and running off in haste with his pack on his back. The symbolic significance was clear to all: even those who had not hitherto suffered at the hands of the enemy power would soon have to flee for their lives. Again, in chapter 24, when his wife dies, we are told that Ezekiel gave no external indication of mourning to show that, when Jerusalem falls to the enemy, the people are not to despair, but instead to keep their confidence in the Lord.

So much for the first factor. But to leave the explanation there would be, I think, to tell only half the story. For, if the truth be told, almost all the great figures in the history of the Christian religion have acted at times very oddly, and in a way that can't just be explained in terms of a conscious, rational decision that this was the best way of getting their point across.

To give but one illustration, Christianity's most popular saint these days is probably St Francis of Assisi, and it is very easy to sympathize with him as portrayed, for example, in the film of his life, *Brother Sun, Sister Moon*. But St Francis was a much more odd character than most modern accounts would have us believe. The contemporary medieval lives are chock-a-block with strange incidents. For example, once when he was being tempted towards material attachments, he ran out naked into the snow and built seven snowmen, and then spent the evening treating them as his family, calling one his wife, and another his daughter, and so on!

All of which leads us to the second and, I think, more profound explanation of Ezekiel's conduct. It is a matter of what it means to be grasped by a religious vision. One of the most intriguing aspects of Ezekiel is the extent to which he was a visionary. At this point it would be natural to recall what is probably the best-known chapter in Ezekiel, chapter 37, the valley of dry bones, when he sees a valley of brittle bones suddenly being brought to life with the sinews being knit together again. But this is by no means an isolated example. The last eight chapters are an extended vision of a purifying worship in the Temple transforming the nation as a whole, with a life-giving stream seen as gushing forth from the Temple building itself. And his book begins with a complex vision of a chariot driven by four strange beasts, in which God sits enthroned, emblazoned in light.

One writer who, I think, understood Ezekiel better than most theologians was the Australian novelist, Patrick White, who won the Nobel Prize for Literature in 1973. In his novel *Riders in the Chariot*, he constructs a story around four individuals, all of whom have at some point in their lives experienced a religious vision, and so, using a metaphor from that first vision of Ezekiel, have become 'Riders in the Chariot'. Throughout the novel, the point White makes is that there are two ways of accepting the visionary ideal that religion holds up before people. On the one hand, one can keep it a safe distance, where its effects are negligible and it is really no more than pie in the sky when you die. Or, on the other hand, one can allow oneself to be grasped by the vision, to be caught up, like Elijah in 2 Kings 2, into the divine chariot, in which case one's perspective will inevitably be totally transformed, and what from the world's perspective is seen as madness will become sanity, and vice versa.

And so it is with all the main characters of the novel. Miss Hare continues to live in a crumbling mansion that is collapsing about her, because she cares about the building and its past. Himmelfarb the Jew allows his fellow workers to beat him up to the point of death because he rejects the use of violence. And Mrs Gumbold, in her single-room shack, continues to care for a husband and family who return her no thanks, because, though they do not care, she does. In each case, the 'sane' solution that the world offers would be to run away from such situations and commitments. But for each of these characters the ideal has become so intensely real that the only possible course for them is to lead a life that the world regards as madness. So the novel ends with Mrs Gumbold being for an instant in the company of the four Living Creatures that drive the chariot, and then, quoting White, 'she lowered her eyes to avoid the dazzle, and walked on breathing heavily for it was still a stiff pull uphill', back to the shed where she would continue to suffer but also continue to care.

It is into just such a framework that Ezekiel fits. For the interesting thing about this prophet is the extent to which everything was conditioned by his vision of the future ideal – so conditioned, in fact, that for him it becomes the life he lives in the present. He was operating at a time of national disaster. The nation was losing its independence, and in the process of becoming an occupied nation, with all its leading citizens deported into exile. Yet, unlike other prophets, Ezekiel does not appeal to God's actions in the past for reassurance, for example, the Exodus or God's covenant with Abraham. Indeed, he may even be the first recorded instance of someone treating the Garden of Eden as a myth (see chapter 28). Instead, everything is seen as dependent on the pure, unmerited kindness of God, an act of pure grace, an invitation from the Rider in the Chariot to join him in his madness.

But, you may say, there is just too high a price to be paid in accepting that invitation, in becoming one of God's lunatics, in allowing the possibility that one might end up acting like Ezekiel or St Francis, or Mrs Gumbold, giving love with none returned.

If this is your worry, let me end by asking if you are certain where madness and sanity really lie. One of the films which has most impressed me in recent years is Werner Herzog's *Fizcarraldo*. Some might detect in its story-line nothing more than the typical lunacy of the Irish! But hair-brained though Fizcarraldo's scheme was – to build an opera house on the Amazon – at least he wanted to bring to the Indians something life-enhancing, something beautiful, whereas, though the realism of the rubber barons certainly brought them employment, it was also at the price of horrendous working conditions. Give me Fizcarraldo's madness any day.

Yet one could ask the question generally about society. The Cold War may be over, but vast stocks of nuclear weapons remain, research continues unabated, and the technology becomes more and more widely diffused. Meantime, some Third World nations spend yet more, vast sums on 'conventional' weapons, with improvements in agriculture taking a poor second place. Everywhere we look, national pride seems to come first. Is that sanity?

Or again, in the modern world abortion has become an acceptable, even normal, form of contraception, and in Britain over two million unborn children have died in this way (since the passing of the 1967 Act). Is that sanity? Or is it perhaps evidence of even greater rationality that the United States can achieve the grand total of a million abortions in a single year?

I could go on. All I will say, is give me God's lunatics any day. Let me into that chariot of Ezekiel's, where there are still ideals, and compassion is the norm. But then, you would scarcely expect any other answer from a Christian, in whose eyes God the Son was just such a lunatic. The crowd accused him of madness even as he was propounding his gospel of love (John 10.20) – love to the loveless, forgiveness to the unforgiving.

Let me into that chariot.

14 ❖ *Liberating*
Law

—

Ezra the priest brought the law before the assembly . . . and the
ears of all the people were attentive

(Neh. 8.2–3 RSV)

In 587 BC the long-expected capture of Jerusalem finally took
place, and the small kingdom of Judah, the remnant of a once
much larger Israel, was no more. But the triumph of the invading
Babylonians was itself to be relatively short-lived. For, a mere fifty
years later, they too were to fall under the rising might of a new
empire, that of the Persians, which at its greatest extent was to
stretch all the way from the borders of India to those of Greece.
One way of managing such a large empire was to allow greater
autonomy to the subject peoples, and so it came about that the
Persians allowed some of the exiled Jerusalem families to return,
and a Jew, Zerubbabel, was appointed governor of a small area
around Jerusalem, roughly twenty miles in radius. His great
achievement was the rebuilding of the Temple, and it is from this
period, at the end of the sixth century, that the writings of the
prophets Haggai and Zechariah come. Both identified Zerubbabel as the Messiah, destined to inaugurate a new, golden age.
However, it was not to be, and the Jews had to wait another full
century, until the period of Ezra and Nehemiah, before events of
truly permanent significance in their history would occur.

This is the context, then, into which we must fit the two books
of these same names. About 440 BC, the Persian king makes
Nehemiah governor, and he is even given permission to refortify
the walls of Jerusalem, presumably against a possible threat from

Egypt. It is, however, the priest Ezra, working a little later, who lies at the real heart of this part of Israel's history – so much so, in fact, that he is often called 'the father of modern Judaism'. This is because, as Nehemiah chapter 8 makes very clear, he sought to place obervation of law at the very centre of what it is to be a Jew, and that is how orthodox Judaism continues to define itself even to this day. No doubt, to some this may seem surprising. After all, was not the Law given to Moses? In one sense that is certainly right, but what one needs to reckon with is the extent to which modern biblical scholarship has made us conscious of a growth in the perceived importance of law. The Book of Leviticus, for instance, with its very detailed rules for daily life, is now commonly thought to date from this post-exilic period, that is to say, from sometime quite close to the period in which Ezra is working.

Yet why such a growth at this time, and, more importantly, what lessons can it teach us? Some readers may already have become impatient with the brief historical outline with which I began, but its relevance surely now becomes clear. With the capture of Jerusalem and the destruction of the first Temple in 587 BC, Jewish identity had been challenged to its very roots. Not only was the monarchy no more, the central symbol of the nation, Solomon's Temple, lay in ruins, and many (particularly the higher echelons of society) had been carried off into exile. Little wonder that Psalm 137 remarks: 'By the waters of Babylon, there we sat down and wept . . . How shall we sing the Lord's song in a foreign land?' (vs. 1, 4 RSV). The fall of Babylon and the rise of Persia had of course given new hope, but it was still such a fragile hope: the grant of a tiny little province compared to King David's once great empire, in its turn insignificant when weighed against the vast territory over which Persia held sway, and anyway, containing only a few of the many exiles scattered throughout the empire. How, then, was Jewish identity to survive? It looked so obviously a lost cause. Yet in the wisdom of God it did survive, even through two thousand years of having no nation state, and all because of what to many must seem an unreasonable dedication to a legal framework for every aspect of life. No longer defined by land but instead by law, a new distinctive identity was forged, and God's people thus lived to tell his praise.

OK, it worked. But can it really have anything to teach us today? Initially, one might think not. So used are we to viewing the Old Testament through the critical spectacles of the New that inevitably what first comes tp mind when we think about law are Jesus' charges against the Pharisees and Paul's equally virulent critique. But that is to focus solely on the abuses, not the reasons why God might have endorsed a proper role for law, for rules, within the scheme of things. So let's reflect further a moment.

One of the great myths of contemporary society is that we are less conformist than our ancestors, that everyone is free to do their own thing. As parents know to their financial cost, the pressures upon children towards conformity are in fact enormous – to get the right set of designer jeans, the appropriate label on one's trainers, and so forth. Nor does the situation change when we reach adulthood. How we decorate our homes, and where we go on holiday have as much to do with the social set with whom we mix as with personal taste. But more insidious still is our attitude to difference. Tolerance is seen as a question of downgrading surviving differences, of saying they just don't matter – you doing your own thing, and I mine. No doubt this sometimes strikes exactly the right chord, but what this modern attitude prevents us from doing is *ever* taking seriously our differences; instead, we exchange polite banalities and fail to understand even why we are committed one way rather than another, far less persuade others of the rightness of our own position. Some at this point may wish to accuse me of intolerance, of committing the last sin left in modern society, the assertion of difference, but that difference is something to which we are called as Christians I emphatically believe; indeed, it seems to me that without such an assertion the Christian faith may not survive.

For right at the heart of Christianity lies a strong claim to difference, to uniqueness: that God became incarnate at one particular time and place in history in one particular individual, Jesus Christ, and that the way to wholeness, the way to health, the way to salvation, lie uniquely through him. That is not to say, of course, that non-Christians or adherents of other religions have no access to the truth or to such health, but surely it is to say that they are still lacking something, and that what they lack matters. So when Christians differ with the surrounding society on questions of worship and prayer, of honesty, or our treatment of the poor, or on abortion or adultery – you name it – all these questions do matter. As Christians we have rebelled against the mindless conformity of modern society, where you are thought of as a failure if you stand out by being conspicuously different, and instead we have a new identity, that given by the community of faith to which we belong. In other words, it is very hard not to end up in some form of conformity (we are all naturally social individuals). So, where rules of belief and behaviour come into their own is in the fact that, just as they ensured the survival of a distinctive identity for the Jews of Ezra's time over against the surrounding culture, so they can do the same for us in our day, and much more.

Now of course within Christianity this sense of being different is much less tied to the notion of law than it was within Judaism; but, even so, let me end by saying something positive in defence of law and rules as a legitimate part of what defines us as different. The secular mind sees law and rules only as a burden, whereas for the perceptive reader of the Bible they can become not only the means of our liberation from mindless conformity, but also liberating in themselves. This is true in at least two respects. First, when we internalize rules, make them truly our own, they do – strange as it initially may seem – indeed cease to be a burden. This is something to which the Old Testament witnesses again and again: 'The law of the Lord is perfect, reviving the soul . . . the precepts of the Lord are right, rejoicing the heart' (Ps. 19.7–8 RSV). Jeremiah even makes this integral to his understanding of a new order: 'I will put my law within them, and I will write it upon their hearts' (Jer. 31.33 RSV). Nor is it hard to comprehend what is meant. Law is only a burden for so long as it is seen as externally imposed. But if our obedience is given to God out of a love that responds to his care and a trust that makes his commands part of our very self, where is the imposition, where the sense of restraint? Whether it be telling the truth, courtesy, remaining loyal to one's marriage vows, saying one's prayers regularly, or whatever example one takes, none need be felt as a burden. All have the potential to be a joy – the more so if one defines one's very identity by such practice and thus makes them a part of one's very self. But failure is of course inevitable, and it is here that we come to our second point. For though we shall certainly fail again and again to live up to those rules, those ideals of our faith, yet balanced against this is the certainty of the ever-open divine embrace of forgiveness that guarantees the transformation of burden into liberation, duty into joy.

In short, then, modern society fails you for being different, for standing out and asserting difference, and the secular temptation for the Church is that it too will follow that course, and simply dwindle away by merging into the society within which it is set. Yet to my mind, Christianity calls us in a very different direction, to the recognition that difference is what gives us our identity; it is a difference that is both enjoyable and endurable, because far from us failing by being different, the very definition of our difference paradoxically largely lies in *failure*: in continuous acceptance of the divine embrace of forgiveness, whenever we fail to reach those ideals, those rules, that law, which God has set before us.

15 ❖ Ethnic Cleansing

—

You shall save alive nothing that breathes
(Deut. 20.16 RSV)

Because the various books of the Bible are bound together as a single volume, it is natural to assume that they are all in complete harmony with one another. Basically, this is true, but not in all cases. The Book of Job, for instance, was written as a challenge to the kind of attitude to suffering that one finds in Kings and Chronicles or some of the psalms: that one's material prosperity or lack of it provided the best guide as to how one stood with God. No, says the author of Job: Job was a good man, yet he suffered appalling misfortunes.

In a similar way, then, it seems likely that the Book of Ruth came to be written as a challenge to what we read elsewhere in the Old Testament. The story tells how Ruth, despite being a Moabitess, supports her Hebrew mother-in-law Naomi, and indeed in due course becomes (as the concluding verses of the book make clear) the great-grandmother of King David. Yet the immediate significance of all this is likely to be lost unless one is also made aware that Moab was one of three small kingdoms lying in what we now call Jordan, and passionately disliked by the Hebrews living on the other side of the Dead Sea. Thus not only are there numerous prophetic oracles against Moab – for instance, in Amos, Isaiah, and Jeremiah – but Deuteronomy 23 even goes so far as to ban for all time any relationship between the two nations: 'No . . . Moabite is to be admitted to the assembly of Yahweh; not even their descendants to the tenth generation may be admitted to the

74

assembly of Yahweh and this is for all time' (v. 3 JB). So here we
have a member of the hated nation not just admitted into the
assembly of Yahweh, but declared to be a direct ancestor of
Israel's greatest king – a clear conflict if there ever was one!

However, the conflict runs much deeper still. The Book of
Deuteronomy is now generally considered to have been written in
the seventh century BC. What the author does is project back into
the mouth of Moses instructions as to how the people are to
behave once they have entered the promised land. Most of its
legislation shows great care and compassion, particularly towards
the marginalized in society, as the book's recurring phrase 'the
stranger, the fatherless and the widow' makes abundantly clear.
But along with that goes an astonishingly relentless ruthlessness
against all foreigners living in the land of Israel. 'In the cities of
these peoples that the Lord your God gives you for an inheritance, you shall save alive nothing that breathes' (Deut. 20.16
RSV). In the area of conquest, women and children were as likely
to be killed as the adult fighting men.

Admittedly, such actions were not advocated just for their own
sake. They were part of a wider strategy: to secure a holy nation, a
people dedicated to God. So chapter 7, though also advocating
such genocide as well as adding a ban on foreign marriages and
requiring the destruction of pagan shrines, concludes by giving as
the reason: 'For you are a people holy to the Lord your God; the
Lord your God has chosen you to be a people for his own possession, out of all the peoples that are on the face of the earth' (v.
6 RSV).

Even so, it is hard to see why such a laudable aim should justify
such doubtful means. More conservative Christians sometimes
talk of God having the right to abrogate the normal rules of
morality in order to achieve his fundamental purposes. But does
that not involve us in paying too high a price in respect of our
understanding of God? It makes God endorse a capricious form
of cruelty – the murder of women and children – which we would
normally regard as putting beyond the pale human perpetrators,

let alone divine. It seems therefore to me a far more plausible approach to think of this as a mere transitional development towards a more balanced understanding of what is meant by God's providential care, one that is no longer defined by race. Yet sadly, it was a lesson only slowly learnt. Even late in the fifth century we find Ezra still requiring the Jews to divorce their foreign wives, including Moabites (chapter 9). Now for such a tiny minority, strangers even in their own land, what could be more natural than an intensification of the attitudes found in Deuteronomy? All was now permitted, it was argued, to preserve the fragile national and religious identity. Even so, protests were not long in being forthcoming, and it is to this period that the Book of Ruth is commonly dated, along with another book containing a similar message, that of Jonah, which tells of a prophet reluctantly called to preach in a foreign land, at Nineveh, the capital of a once-deadly ancient foe, the Assyrians. Both these writings of course helped prepare for the Christian dispensation in which race ceased to be a relevant criterion.

That said, it would be very easy at this point to conclude in self-congratulation: that the Christian Church has nothing in common with these early primitive Hebrew attitudes. We have learnt the lesson of tolerance, so surely we can happily close those chapters of the Bible? On the contrary, it seems to me that that would be quite the wrong inference to draw. Because human beings continue to make fundamentally the same mistakes throughout their history, we need to be constantly reminded and forewarned of how our ancestors in the faith went wrong. However, it is not just a matter of that negative lesson; positive conclusions may also be identified. For me, those early attitudes of Israel have two vital lessons for us today.

The first is the necessity for sympathetic understanding. Amid all the national turmoil that is taking place in eastern Europe, it has been fascinating to observe what little sympathy has been shown by English public opinion towards the armed struggles of Ossetians, Armenians, Croats, Serbs, Bosnians, and so forth.

English national identity has been secure for so long that there seems no consciousness of what a tenuous thing such identity can be, when it has been perhaps submerged for hundreds of years, as was so often the case in eastern Europe. Like many of the small nations of eastern Europe, Israel lay in the cross-fire between two great powers on either side, and presumably one major reason for suspicion of another small nation (such as nearby Moab) was the worry that, though speaking a common language (Hebrew), Moab could not always be relied upon to take the same side – and indeed, might use Israel's disadvantage to further its own ends. Centuries later we have a similar explanation for the conduct of Croatia and Serbia. Though speaking the same language (Serbo-Croat), more often than not in their history they have been on opposed sides, all as part of a life-and-death struggle to preserve their ethnic identity. Of course, none of this justifies the ruthless, barbaric measures that have so often been employed in the process, but it surely takes us at least some way towards comprehending the attitude of the author of Deuteronomy, or its modern equivalent in the so-called 'ethnic cleansing' that is now taking place in former Yugoslavia. The ultimate perceived danger both then and now was of the nation disappearing not just for a while (which was bad enough), but perhaps for ever – which is exactly what happened to Moab.

But secondly, and perhaps more importantly, it reminds us that communal identity never comes cheaply. Even when the Church abolished the criterion of race, agonizing decisions still had to be made as to what constituted orthodoxy and what heresy. The Inquisition and heresy trials have long since gone, but we should not kid ourselves that such tests are no longer, and need no longer, be made. Admittedly, almost everything can be found on the Church's eccentric fringe, but that is surely still quite different from legitimating it as part of the episcopal bench or assigning it a role in shaping the Church's liturgy or official teaching. For, however open the Church tries to be to those of little belief or none, if it is to survive as a community it must have an identity, and that means at times making unpleasant decisions about what does or does not constitute the true nature of faith, what is and what is not acceptable behaviour among its members, and so forth.

So by all means let us endorse the message of compassion and tolerance given by the Book of Ruth, but let us also not lose sight of the realism of that earlier history, flawed though it may be. A tolerance of indifference is worth nothing at all. As Christians we are summoned to a much more difficult task. Yes, to be outward-looking, yes, to respect the integrity of those with whom we disagree, but also to add a clear recognition that what we believe and do as Christians is no mere optional extra, but constitutive of the very identity of the community of which we are part.

16 ✤ A Questioning Faith

—

Master, who did sin, this man, or his parents, that he was
born blind?

(John 9.2 AV)

With all those heroes and saints of the faith who have paid the
final sacrifice of their own lives, it is very easy to jump to the
conclusion that Christianity is all about absolute commitment
with never a doubt upon the way. Indeed, this conviction can
often be reinforced by churches or parishes where belief in Bible
or creed is treated as the essential litmus test for being part of that
community. But, as so often in history, the reality turns out to be
rather more complex, and it is to that more complex reality that I
wish now to draw your attention: a reality in which doubt and
questioning characterize even the Bible itself.

To illustrate this, I want to consider with you three books which
are commonly thought to date from somewhere in the post-exilic
period (no one is sure precisely when) – Chronicles, Ecclesiastes,
and Job. Certainly, the concern of all three with the issue of how
far we can detect for ourselves a divine order and justice in the
world must have seemed highly pertinent to such a community in
the throes of suffering and oppression. But of course they were
not the first to raise the issue. Centuries earlier, the question had
already been posed: if God is really just, will he not reward those
who obey his commands and punish those who do not? This is a
natural assumption, and one that many today would say continues
to hold true, once one takes into account the next life. For ancient Israel, though, the question was much more fraught, since

79

for most of its history it had no belief in life after death; so any such correlation between merit and reward either had to happen in this life or not at all.

That there was such a correspondence is exactly the viewpoint we find in many of the psalms. Consider, for instance, the extraordinary confidence of Psalm 37: 'Fret not yourself because of the wicked, be not envious of wrongdoers! For they will soon fade like the grass, and wither like the green herb' (vs. 1–2 RSV). Indeed, the author even goes on to declare: 'I have been young, and now am old; yet I have not seen the righteous forsaken or his children begging bread' (v. 25). Nor was this by any means an uncommon attitude. It is also an assumption that dominates much of the historical writing within the Old Testament, with the two books of Kings being a particularly good example. The narrative repeatedly drums home the moral lesson that those kings who 'did evil in the sight of the Lord' received their just deserts, while those few who did good were blessed by him.

Or rather, almost so. For there are two glaring exceptions where the author's theology did not quite fit the facts: the wicked seventh-century BC king Manasseh, who none the less reigned for fifty-four years, and the good king Josiah, who died on the battlefield of Megiddo in 609 BC, aged a mere thirty-nine. The best that the author can offer is that Josiah paid the price for his grandfather's sins. But will that do? Other writers in the Old Testament are sure that it won't. They doubt what Kings is telling us and wrestle with the question of how merit and reward are really related. Three very different approaches are the result. Each has much to teach us about ourselves.

Take first the author of Chronicles, the Chronicler. Here we have the ancient equivalent of the fundamentalist, determined to plug the gaps, however implausible the result. So whereas Kings is at least loyal to the historical facts, the Chronicler argues that Manasseh must in reality have repented in order to have enjoyed such a long reign, and Josiah must really have done something wrong to have suffered such a tragically early death. Accordingly,

80

a divine command to be disobeyed is duly provided for the latter (2 Chron. 35.21) and a prayer of penitence for the former (2 Chron. 33.12). Not that this was all bad. It eventually generated the beautiful prayer of Manasseh which we find in the Apocrypha. However, the negative side of the coin was the way in which such a theology continued to trap people into an implausible view of the world, forcing them to see belief in such correspondence between merit and fate as a test of their faith when it was no such thing. Look up, for instance, Psalm 73. The author is in agony, has almost lost his faith, as he desperately tries to hold on to this conviction of a congruence between merit and reward. By the end of the psalm he declares that he has succeeded, but one wonders what contortions he has had to go through to keep loyal to what his community seems to have required of him. And are we not aware of numerous, similar contortions going on today, with individuals struggling to hold on to beliefs that they think God requires of them when they could so easily be liberated by having their horizons widened, by following their questions wheresoever they lead?

But I do mean *follow* the question. For if one plague of our modern world is the closed mind of fundamentalism, another equally pernicious is a laid-back agnosticism that fails to take the question seriously at all. That approach also finds its representative in the Bible, in the Book of Ecclesiastes. Not of course that the author disbelieved in God – he makes his belief quite clear. But it is combined with a deep agnosticism about how much we can know of the divine purposes. Even his most famous chapter, chapter 3, is often misread. For when he declares that 'for everything there is a season . . . a time to be born, and a time to die' and so on, it might sound as though he is suggesting that everything is under the controlling, caring hand of God. Yet, if one reads to the end of the chapter, one discovers that the truth is quite otherwise. For he goes on to declare that, though God knows such appropriate times, he has hidden them from human sight, and so we might as well behave as though they did not exist!

So, if the Chronicler illustrates the closed mind of the fundamentalist, the 'Preacher' (as the author of Ecclesiastes is sometimes known) equally well portrays the lazy mind of the agnostic:
the person who gives up the struggle, the questioning, almost
before it has begun. Now contrast both with the author of the
Book of Job. On the one hand, the approach of the Chronicler is
ridiculed on page after page, as Job's friends try in vain plausibly
to apply traditional theology to the dreadful suffering that has
befallen their friend. Yet, on the other, Job is not allowed to rest
content with the agnosticism of the Preacher. He demands that
God show himself, that he display something of his concern for
him. For example, chapter 10: 'I will give free utterance to my
complaint . . . I will say to God, Do not condemn me; let me know
why thou dost contend against me' (vs. 1–2 RSV). Or again, chapter 23: 'Oh, that I knew where I might find [God], that I might
come even to his seat! I would lay my case before him . . . Would
he contend with me in the greatness of his power? No; he would
give heed to me' (vs. 3–6 RSV). Then at long last his wrestling and
his searching meet with an appropriate response in God's speech
from the whirlwind (chapter 38). His yearning and longing for
God have at last their due reward.

Yet note carefully what the Book of Job promises and what it
does not. It promises that if we wrestle seriously with our doubts, if
we really long to deepen our knowledge of God, then God will
indeed carry us further along that path beyond the doubt. What is
emphatically not promised, though, is the definitive answer. By
comparison with the New Testament treatment on suffering, the
answer of the Book of Job is distinctly superficial and un-
enlightening. But at least it prepared the way for the New Testament by once and for all exposing the absurdities of the point
from which its doubts began.

Three responses to doubt, then, all from within the Bible itself:
a desperate plugging of the gaps as with the closed mind of the
Chronicler; lazy resignation and abandonment of further thought
as with the Preacher; or – surely the only possible model for us –

the wrestling Job, who won through at the last to a deeper knowledge and trust. We all know that that must be the right answer, but when we try honestly to face ourselves, which one are we really – Chronicler, Preacher or Job? A hard question, but upon which much may depend – perhaps even our salvation.

17 ✤ The Need to Dream

—

Where there is no vision, the people perish
(Prov. 29.18 AV)

The Book of Daniel in the Old Testament and Revelation in the New are representative of a particular type of literature, known to biblical scholars as apocalyptic. Indeed, in the United States the Book of Revelation is commonly called the Apocalypse. In everyday language these days, we tend to use the words 'apocalypse' and 'apocalyptic' to mean dramatic events which are seen as taking place at the end of time, and that is certainly true of the way the Book of Revelation tells its story. However, among biblical scholars the words are used rather more widely: of any writings that use the imagery of angels and demons and so forth to describe the inauguration by God of a totally new golden age, and that best describes the Book of Daniel.

But, whether we take a gentler version like Daniel or the Book of Revelation in all its gruesomeness, the sad truth is that most Christians find the presence of this kind of material in the Bible acutely embarrassing – all those weird descriptions of strange beasts, and devils and angels fighting it out in a heavenly battlefield. Even Cranmer, when producing the Prayer Book lectionary, decided to exclude most of the Book of Revelation from the list of daily readings – the only book in the Bible to be given this treatment by him. This is true also of modern compilers of readings. Thus, for instance, the Alternative Service Book recommends only three passages from Daniel for its Sunday readings, those concerning the three friends in the fiery furnace, the hero in the lions' den, and, last but by no means least, its magnificent description of God as the Ancient of Days in chapter 7 (vs. 9–14). That being so, it would not be strange if some readers were rather surprised by my opening identification of the book's contents with those of Revelation. Yet a quick glance at its last three chapters, with the Archangel Michael busily engaged fighting it out with the angels of Persia and Greece, would soon confirm the appropriateness of the comparison, and also with it their shared problematic character.

But the difficulties are there to be faced. So let us face head-on the challenge of what on earth we are to do with such books. Should we, for instance, follow the advice given to me by a chemistry master at school? An otherwise devout Christian, he told me that the book of Revelation must have got into the Bible by mistake; not only was it nonsense, but it must have been written under the influence of drugs! Or should we perhaps go to the other extreme, that of the conservative or fundamentalist Christian, who by comparing the material with what is happening in the world today, tries to argue that the world will indeed soon end in the manner predicted. For instance, it was until very recently a popular ploy among American television evangelists to say that the world would shortly conclude in a nuclear war between the Soviet Union and the United States, and that all this could be discovered from careful scrutiny of the biblical text.

No, neither side is right. If you want to understand what is going on, I suggest that we reflect for a moment on a verse from Proverbs: 'Where there is no vision, the people perish' (29.18 AV). For what seems to me to be the single, most important thing about this type of literature is its visionary dream-like quality, and, no matter how implausible it may seem at first, if we think further about the nature of day-dreaming and the role it plays in our lives, then we will be well on our way to understanding the religious point of such books.

First, then, think of the curious blend of fact, fiction, and fantasy that constitutes our dreams, whether they be night-visions or during the day. We are all creatures of such limited imagination that unless there are at least some strong points of contact with present reality, the dream would not be able to get off the ground at all. So on those occasions when we wake up and can remember what occurred – rare, in my case – what we always find is some point of departure in everyday truth that has helped to make the whole fantastic picture plausible – at least for so long as the dream lasted! And much the same can happen in our day-dreams. We build our fantasies on a casual remark that has become a great work of praise, or a fleeting look into which we have read mutual sexual interest.

Now, if we examine in detail the Book of Daniel, what we find is exactly this same blend of fact, fiction, and fantasy. It claims to be visions of the future granted to someone called Daniel writing in the sixth century BC. But the only time it touches earth, as it were, is in chapter 11, where it gives a detailed and accurate account of events in the second century BC. Of still later events, it is inaccurate, such as the predicted death of Antiochus Epiphanes, the Seleucid King of Syria, which did not take place in Israel as foretold. But, more surprisingly, there are similar inaccuracies about earlier events – and to an extraordinary degree. For example, Belshazzar is portrayed as the successor and son of Nebuchadnezzar, though in fact he was the son of Nabonid and never formally reigned as king. Again, the story of Nebuchadnezzar turning into a beast and eating grass seems to be based on an incident in the life of Nabonid – correctly attributed, for example, in the Dead Sea Scrolls. Or, to give one last and very glaring example, there never seems to have been a king called Darius the Mede; and in fact there is no room for him between the last of the Chaldean kings and Cyrus the Persian who had conquered the Medes.

In the case of the Book of Revelation, the very few historical allusions seem accurate enough, but there is equally this strange combination of fact, fiction, and fantasy, perhaps most obviously noticeable in the visual impossibility of so many of its descriptions.

If you try to picture them, they quickly become absurd or comic, and indeed this is well illustrated by the most famous attempt to do so: the marvellous fourteenth-century Apocalypse Tapestry preserved at Angers on the Loire in northern France. Probably the most remarkable thing about that tapestry, apart from its beauty, is the extent to which the images have had to be simplified in order to tell a visually coherent tale.

And so at last I come to the religious point behind such dreams. Both books were written at a time when the communities to which they were addressed were at a very low ebb. Both seem to have been undergoing persecution, in the one case from King Antiochus Epiphanes (175–64 BC) and in the other from the Emperor Domitian (AD 81–96). They were therefore written to assure their readers of a better future, one in which God's will would ultimately triumph; and it is really this message that matters, not the details of the picture. That is what God wanted to convey through the writer, not detailed advance information about the future course of history.

But, you may well object, why all the irrelevant details? Why did God not just give a general assurance that the ultimate victory was secure? It is at this point that one must take into account the way in which our waking dreams crucially affect the way in which we behave in the present. A Polish journalist friend once offered me a dramatic illustration of this. Some experiments on rats were conducted in his native land, and one fact to emerge was that if a rat is placed in a vat of water with steep sides, it will swim around desperately trying to escape but be dead within a few hours from exhaustion. However, if you place a piece of wood in the water and allow the rat to lay hold of it for a little while and then withdraw it, that same rat that would have been dead within a couple of hours from exhaustion can now keep on swimming for as long as twenty-five hours. Such is the difference that a specific hope, a definite vision of the future, can make. And though no doubt it is somewhat invidious to compare ourselves with rats, much the same can be said of human beings.

The examples are legion, but if you want a specific non-biblical example, think of the event which Sir Walter Scott regarded as decisive for his own development. The story is told that he was a bit of a dunce at school, and very shy and timid. However, one day, when he was twelve, he was present at an occasion at which Robert Burns was being entertained. The poet noticed a couplet from a poem inscribed at the foot of a painting hanging on the wall, and asked for the author. None of the adults knew, but the young Scott not only managed to give the answer, but even completed the poem. Burns was so delighted that he told Scott that one day he would be a great writer, and from that day Scott began to dream, and sure enough, one day the dream became a reality.

Or, if you prefer a more ecclesiastical example, Randall Davidson in his biography of Alexander Campbell Tait informs us that once when Tait was a boy walking through Lambeth Palace, he informed his parents that one day he would live there – which to no small degree surprised them as the entire family were at that time all Scots Presbyterians. But sure enough, the boy's day-dream eventually became true in 1868.

In other words, it is often only because we dream of an 'impossible' future that the future then becomes possible and turns itself into a reality. Imagine how different their history might have been had Scott and Tait simply remained realists. Scott would just have accepted the judgement of his teachers; Tait that of his Scottish inheritance.

In fact, hoping for much enables much to happen. God of course knows that – that is the way he made us. And that is why he has so often helped our ancestors in the faith to dream, and to dream especially in periods of trial – in order to make a very different future possible. For it is a sad fact of life that those who expect little, who dream little, in reality do little and receive little.

And that is exactly what we see to be the case with regard to both Daniel and the Book of Revelation – that dreaming much achieved much. In the context in which the Book of Daniel was written, what the author offers his readers must have seemed to an impartial observer of events an utterly absurd dream. Not only was the present persecution to cease, but the day would come when all those empires that had for so long dominated Jewish history would collapse, including even the tyrannical regimes that had resulted from the conquests of Alexander the Great in the Middle East; instead, a Jew was to reign on God's behalf over all the world. As Christians we might legitimately see the last element in his hope coming true in the coming of Christ and the spreading of the gospel throughout the world. But this is secondary to the main point that I want to make, which is this: it was only because Daniel preserved the fire of hope in adverse conditions that the dream of a better future could at last succeed in dawning. Without such a book, Judaism would have long since disappeared as a distinctive religion.

Much the same applies to the Book of Revelation. How was it possible that Christianity, an obscure Jewish sect, would within three centuries become the official religion of the Roman Empire? It would be naïve of course to provide a single explanation, but I venture to suggest that a large element in that eventual success was an apocalyptic mood, as it were: daring to dream the impossible, as does the Book of Revelation, and indeed many other early Christian writings, such as the Shepherd of Hermas, the Didache, Irenaeus, and so forth.

What finally of ourselves, though? Have we as Christians forgotten how to dream? Has the contemporary Church become so preoccupied with what is feasible, what it can afford and so forth, that it has lost its sense of vision, and thus its ability to inspire? And, if so, is that not a terrible indictment upon a Church that Luke claims in Acts was founded in fulfilment of a prophecy in the Book of Joel which promises: 'and your young men shall see visions and your old men shall dream dreams' (Acts 2.17; Joel 2.28 RSV)?

Ah, once more to dream, and what then?

✤ Part Three ✤
Gospel
Hidden Treasure

18 ❖ Surprised
by Joshua

—

'But who do you say that I am?' Peter answered him. 'You are
the Christ'

(Mark 8.29 RSV)

Were I to begin by declaring that Christians gather to worship
Joshua the Messiah, quite a few readers would, I suspect, feel
rather confused. Yet the explanation is quite simple. For all I have
done is to translate from Greek into Hebrew the central Christian
affirmation: 'I believe in Jesus Christ'. 'Jesus' is the Greek version
of the Hebrew name 'Joshua', and 'Christ' is the Greek form of
the Hebrew title 'Messiah'. Yet behind that simple change lies a
multitude of meaning. For describing our Lord thus helps us to
highlight what is often forgotten: how deeply surprising, not to
say shocking, Jesus' life and message were to his contemporaries.

Take the name 'Joshua' first. It seems to have been common
enough in first-century Palestine, and so at one level we need look
no further than that for Mary's and Joseph's choice of their son's
name. But in those days the etymologies of names were taken with
great seriousness, and so, not surprisingly, at the beginning of
Matthew's Gospel we find an angel instructing Joseph to call the
child 'Jesus' because of its popular etymology, that the name
meant 'God Saves'. It was of course a meaning that was to be fully
justified by the subsequent course of events.

In drawing attention to this etymology as many an early Christian writer observed, Matthew (almost certainly) intended that we
should call to mind the most famous person in the Old Testament
to bear the same name. For just as Joshua took over from Moses to

93

lead the Israelites into the promised land, so Jesus, the new Joshua, also marks the inauguration of a new era, a new testament or covenant: one whereby he too leads us into a promised land, but one no longer narrowly confined to the Palestinian littoral or coastal strip, but rather constituted by a new vision for this entire world and the next. Indeed, the parallel is reinforced in Matthew's Gospel by the Holy Family returning from Egypt after the massacre of the innocents (2.13–15). For, as you may well recall, though Moses led the people out of Egypt, he was denied entry into the promised land, and it was Joshua to whom this task was entrusted (Deut. 1.37–38). Now, presumably the argument runs, here is another, though greater, Joshua. But what a different Joshua – a child of peace, not a man of war!

And what of the title 'Christ' or 'Messiah'? What are we to make of that? In the form we now have the gospel story, the title appears entirely unproblematic. Indeed, precisely because it was the most frequent way that his disciples described Jesus, it came to be used of them also (Acts 11.26), and eventually degenerated into what we have now, its use as little more than a 'surname' for him. However, it was not always so. Not only does Mark make Peter's declaration 'Thou art the Christ' in chapter 8 the pivot around which his entire Gospel revolves, he closely links it with a transformed understanding of when the term may appropriately apply – even in the acceptance of suffering (vs. 27–33). Similarly, Matthew (24.23–25) cautions against too facile an identification of the returning Christ. The meaning of the term is thus crucial. But what does it mean?

At one level, the answer is quickly given. It simply means 'the anointed one', but what does this anointing signify? That is the more difficult question, but also the more rewarding, because what we discover is not only the notion of messiahship transformed, but along with it, priest, prophet, and king.

Oil (or to give it its technical name, *chrism*) was used symbolically in the Old Testament to commission individuals for key roles in the divine plan of salvation, and so we find such oil used to anoint kings, priests, and prophets. Of these the best known is the anointing of kings, specifically referred to in the case of Saul, David, and Solomon. It is a practice that has continued to this day, as in the anointing of our own Queen at her coronation in June 1953.

Almost certainly, though, the practice was borrowed from the older tradition of anointing priests, though some scholars insist that the influence was the other way round. At all events, Exodus 29, in describing the ordination of priests, insists upon their anointing with oil; and Psalm 133 has a marvellous description of this. This moving psalm runs thus: 'Behold, how good and pleasant it is when brothers dwell in unity! It is like the precious oil upon the head, running down upon the beard, upon the beard of Aaron, running down on the collar of his robes!' (vs. 1–2 RSV). Clearly, the oil was used in generous measure! But in one's amusement at the messiness of the image, do not lose the point of the analogy. When we live together in unity, the author is declaring, we feel graced, blessed by God; and that sense of grace, sense of blessing, is as great as that given to the priest by God when he is made his agent in ordination. It is an overflowing grace, not a dribble, but one that pours over him in abundance.

Then finally, more rarely, there is the anointing of the prophet. Thus in 1 Kings 19 Elijah is instructed not only to anoint a couple of new kings, but also 'Elisha . . . you shall anoint to be prophet in your place' (v. 16 RSV).

And so gradually from this notion of the anointed one as someone especially commissioned by God, whether king, priest, or prophet, there arose a much stronger sense, not just of *an* anointed one, but of *the* anointed one, the one person uniquely commissioned by God for a specific task, and it is this person with whom Jesus is being identified in the Gospels.

When precisely the terminology became fixed in this way is rather hard to determine. Certainly as early as the sixth century BC, when the small southern remnant of David's empire, now called Judah, began to collapse, people looked back to the glorious days of four centuries previously; and spoke of a future son of David who would inaugurate a new age of divine blessing, and this idea is reflected in prophets like Jeremiah and Ezekiel. Yet neither of these prophets call this future king the Messiah. However, within a few generations we have the prophets Haggai and Zechariah confidently identifying two of their own contemporaries as Messiahs. Zerubbabel, the grandson of the last reigning king, is identified as the royal Messiah, and Joshua, the High-Priest, as the priestly Messiah – the one commissioned to restore the nation's military fortunes, the other the Temple devastated by the invading Babylonians. However, their hopes were soon dashed, and so expectations of a future Messiah to redeem the nation's fortunes continued to grow, as is reflected, for instance, in the second-century Book of Daniel (9.25) with its reference to the renewal of Jerusalem under a future 'anointed' one.

Yet it would be a mistake to deduce from this that very precise conceptions had been formed by the time of Jesus. Rather, what seems to have been the case is that messianic expectations characterized the beliefs of only some of the people, and even then there was wide divergence in what exactly was envisaged. Thus the community at Qumran, about which we know so much as a result of the discovery of the Dead Sea Scrolls in 1947, seems to have anticipated – like the prophets Haggai and Zechariah – two Messiahs, a royal and a priestly one, and some of the community perhaps even three, with a prophetic one thrown in as well.

At Advent and Christmas Carol Services we are accorded the great advantage of hindsight. The result is that it is very easy for us to suppose that there was an inevitable and obvious progression through the Old Testament that culminated in the first coming of our Lord. Yet the truth is quite otherwise. Expectations of the future Messiah were, as we have seen, thoroughly confused, and indeed people were not even certain how many of them there would be! But, in so far as they were certain, what they looked forward to was the restoration of an old order, what were seen as the days of the nation's military and spiritual greatness under

David. Is it any wonder that Jesus, with his very different sense of his mission, responds to Peter's confession 'Thou art the Christ' shortly afterwards with the words 'Get behind me, Satan'?

So only slowly does Jesus accept this title of himself, as he tries first to re-educate his disciples as to what being God's anointed might involve. And just think for a moment of the dramatic transformation that he does effect. Instead of the Old Testament Joshua who did not hesitate even to use genocide as part of his programme for the liberation of the land (cf. Josh. 9.24), here we have the New Testament Jesus excluding no one, but instead extending his loving care to all, including even the hated occupying power, the Romans, and the despised neighbour, the Samaritans. Again, instead of the empire of David and Solomon which included most of present-day Jordan, Syria and Lebanon, his messianic kingdom was to be a kingdom without frontiers, a kingdom proclaimed on a cross, as the penitent thief so clearly recognized: 'remember me when you come into your kingdom' (Luke 23.42 JB). Again, instead of a resplendent and purified temple, this priestly Messiah inaugurated a temple of his body: 'Destroy this temple and I shall rebuild it in three days'. In other words, the priest was also the sacrificial victim, the one who brought new life to us all not through an exclusivist cult, but by dying in order that we might live, by opening the way of love to all. Then finally, there was the prophetic Messiah, the one who spoke as a prophet, yet not as one of the prophets, who spoke with a new authority, challenging both by his teaching and his life what till then had been perceived as the will of God: 'Ye have heard . . . but I say unto you' (Matt. 5.21–22 etc. AV).

Thus we should not be surprised that so many of the Jews of Jesus' day found it a message impossible to accept: there was just too much in their history that was being challenged. To us, the passages that point in this direction, such as the four sections in Isaiah that speak of the suffering servant, have assumed such prominence that we tend to think the development from the Old Testament to the New inevitable, but it was anything but. The life and teaching of Jesus revolutionized the way in which the notion of Messiah was understood.

What, then, does all this say to us? Does it not warn us of the danger of assuming that our faith is a sort of package deal with everything sown up in advance? Many in Jesus' day got it radically wrong; might not we also, unless we remain open to the possibility of change, to the possibility of fresh promptings of the Holy Spirit?

But, you may ask, could such major changes continue to happen in the subsequent history of the Church after the New Testament canon was closed? Most certainly – and they did. To give a couple of examples at random, once the Church became the official religion of the empire, it found it necessary to abandon pacifism as a universal strategy not because it saw Jesus' teaching about turning the other cheek as now irrelevant, but because it saw that it was one thing to do that in a situation where only one's own interests were threatened, quite another where the welfare of others was concerned. Or again, there was Luther's major discovery at the Reformation that justification is not something that we do, but something that God does for us, with all the implications that had for the Church's practice. Likewise, today fresh issues and challenges present themselves – such as feminism, the presence of other faiths in our midst, or the transformed understanding of the Bible that modern biblical studies has brought with it. In none of these cases are the conclusions to be drawn wholly clear. But why fear? Transformation and change have always been part of the history of the community of faith.

There is not the time to expand on these examples. Instead, let me leave you with a solitary instance from the Old Testament that anticipated the revolution in the understanding of 'anointed' that was to follow. Chapter 45 of Isaiah opens with the identification of no less a figure than the conquering Persian king, Cyrus, as the Lord's 'anointed'. God does not always work in the ways we expect. Some of the Jews of Jesus' time failed to learn the lesson. Have we?

19 ❖ *Where Does It Hurt?*

—

Examine yourselves, to see whether you are holding to your faith
(2 Cor. 13.5 RSV)

These days a frequent accusation against Christian belief is that it amounts to no more than a product of one's environment. Had we been born in India, we would have been a Hindu, in Iran, a Muslim. In one sense, that is of course true. But what is often forgotten is that it is a feature which applies to all our beliefs and actions, not just religion. Inevitably our education, the community to which we belong, and so forth, all help to shape the way we think. Even the atheist is not immune. For how he or she perceives their atheism will very much depend on what they are reacting against – Rome, chapel, or whatever!

The important issue is thus not the conditioning – that is inevitable – but whether we are able to point to ways in which we are more than just our environment, more than just our prejudices. Is our religion a genuine search for the truth? What does it say about ourselves, if we only use it as a whip with which to lash others of whom we disapprove, or if we rule out of court its application to key areas of our lives such as politics?

Nor should we exclude the Gospels themselves from such questions. Occasionally, there would seem little alternative to admitting that the writers fail us. For instance, so traumatic have Matthew and John clearly found the split with Judaism that John indifferently calls all Jesus' opponents 'the Jews', as though the whole race were opposed to him, while it is in Matthew's Gospel that we find the horrific verse that was to be used to justify centuries of persecution: 'His blood be on us and on our children' (27.25 RSV).

Yet on the other side may be set one exciting discovery of modern biblical studies: the remarkable extent to which the evangelists seek to transcend the limitations of their environment. In their search for the truth they do not hesitate to raise questions, often as disturbing for themselves as for us. To illustrate this, let us consider how our first three Gospels came to be written.

Most scholars are agreed that Matthew, Mark, and Luke are part of a shared tradition, unlike John who, while he may have known the others, uses sources unique to himself to strike an independent note. The consensus is that Mark was written first, and that Matthew and Luke then used Mark to write their own Gospels, but supplemented his account not just with information of their own, but also with much material drawn from a now lost Gospel, known as Q (from the first letter of the German word for source). Because they are thus part of a shared tradition, the normal way of referring to the first three Gospels is as 'the Synoptic Gospels', from the Greek work which means seeing things from the same point of view. However, to describe the situation thus is in fact highly misleading. All three are very different in their emphases, and indeed it would be a great tragedy if we did not have all three.

Considering that Mark was the first Gospel to be written, one might have thought that it would be powerfully reassuring in the good news it brings. But not a bit of it! It is almost as though Mark takes a perverse pleasure in adding uncertainty to uncertainty, mystery upon mystery. Thus Jesus appears without explanation on stage, already as a grown adult, preaching that the Kingdom of God is at hand. Yet we are given next to no information regarding what this kingdom is about, apart from the fact that it will require repentance for our sins, and that in Jesus' person it is coming with great authority and great power. For as Mark records, everything normally beyond human control obeys him – the wind, the waters, and the demons (who were then thought of as lying behind so much illness). But who is this puzzling figure with such power?

Mark offers us no clear, unambiguous answer. Thus the strange title, Son of Man, is left unexplained, and the central declaration of Jesus as the Christ right at the mid-point of the Gospel is almost immediately undermined as having any simple, straightforward meaning by Jesus' response: 'Get behind me Satan! (8.33 RSV). Then comes the horrific death of this man of power, followed by a mysteriously incomplete resolution. For, while he records Jesus' triumph over death in the sense that he mentions the empty tomb, his Gospel originally ended abruptly at 16.8 without any mention of the resurrection appearances (normally indicated by a separate paragraph or footnote in modern translations). Instead, he simply records how 'trembling and astonishment had come upon them; and they said nothing to any one, for they were afraid' (RSV). It is perhaps little wonder that a later editor felt it necessary to add a brief account of the resurrection itself.

No doubt part of the explanation of all this air of mystery was to encourage the non-believer to seek further explanation from within the resurrection community itself. So enigmatically is Jesus presented that one cannot but want to know more. Yet I suspect that Mark's strategy was also aimed at his fellow Christians, and thus indirectly at ourselves. For of all the Gospels, Mark's is the most open-ended. There are so many loose ends, unresolved issues. Might he not be teasing us towards living in trust, accepting uncertainty? Security, wanting to know exactly where we are, is a very basic human desire, but Mark will have none of it. Even the best of us will fail (hence all that stress on Peter's repeated failures). All we can do is pick ourselves up once more, and live expectantly, awaiting God's new future to dawn. And might that not be why there are no resurrection appearances? We are not to try to secure ourselves with some reference to the past. We are to live with our eyes firmly set on the future, no matter how ambiguous the present may appear to be.

Whether Mark thereby undermined a personal desire of his own for security, we do not know. Certainly it is a temptation to which we all sometimes succumb – of trusting more in the medium than in the message, of securing ourselves by what we can see or hear than through Christ himself. So Mark might well have been suspicious of all that additional definition and security provided by the expansion of his text that Matthew and Luke undertake. Yet, unlike so many modern perspectives, they also see it as essential that the gospel message should challenge themselves and their community, not simply endorse it.

Let us take Luke first. Luke was a Gentile who wrote both the Gospel of that name and Acts, and one of the things he is very much concerned to stress is the natural development of the community beyond the bounds of Israel. Indeed, so concerned is he about this that he omits all reference to the resurrection appearances in Galilee to which both Matthew and the editor of Mark refer, and instead he only includes those that occur in Jerusalem itself (the existence of such appearances is independently attested by John). The reason for the omission appears to be to ensure that the Gospel will be seen as having a natural progression – from Jesus' ministry on the fringes of Israel, in northern Galilee, to the capital Jerusalem, and from there out to the Roman world as a whole, as he relates in Acts.

From all that I have observed so far, it might seem that Luke would come under precisely the same sort of charge as I have already levelled at so many modern perspectives on Jesus: that they simply endorse the writer's present perspective. That, I think, is true. For Luke, as we have already noted was a Gentile, and his Gospel is in fact dedicated to a fellow-Gentile, called Theophilus. So, in endorsing so heavily the move into the Gentile world, Luke isn't producing anything particularly challenging. However, that is by no means the end of the story. For what is intriguing about Luke's Gospel is the way in which he insists that the Christian community is opened by Jesus not just to the Gentiles, but to all people, no matter how repellent or marginal they might seem. Thus, while Matthew opens his Gospel with the visit of the wise men with their expensive gifts, Luke opens his with the visit of the poor shepherds, and when one hears the list of incidents and teaching of this kind unique to Luke, one cannot help but suspect that a point of really major importance is being made – for example, the Parable of the Prodigal Son (15.11–24), the Good Samaritan (10.29–37), the story of the rich man and Lazarus (16.19–31), and the story of the penitent thief on the cross (23.39–43), all these are unique to Luke. Again, while Matthew and Mark record the story of the woman who anointed Jesus' head, it is to Luke that we owe the story of the sinner who washes his feet with her tears (7.38).

Luke himself was a physician and relatively well-to-do. The addressee of his Gospel is called 'most excellent Theophilus'. The only other person so described in his two books is a Roman provincial governor. So the probability is that it is one relatively privileged person in the Roman Empire addressing another. But, if so, note what happens. Luke does not simply assure Theophilus that he is now part of what was once an exclusively Jewish community, he also challenges him to view all the despised of the Empire as just as much called to be part of this Church – women of dubious morals, the poor, criminals, and so forth. Indeed, if one compares Luke's account of the healing of the centurion's servant with that of Matthew, one discovers that Luke has carefully re-written the story to emphasize the need of even an imperial administrator for the mediation of this despised subject people, the Jews (Luke 7.3 has no parallel in Matthew's version at 8.5). Not only that, but Jesus' Kingdom is promised on the cross to, of all people, a convicted thief. Certainly, no easy gospel here for the middle-class Luke or the upper-class Theophilus.

Matthew's perspective also produces unease, but for a very different reason. Here we have a Jew writing for fellow-Jews. The author was obviously not the apostle called Matthew – for why then would he have needed to use other Gospels as sources, Mark and Q? The reason why this Gospel is none the less called Matthew is because alone of all the evangelists he substitutes Matthew instead of Levi as the name of the publican or tax-gatherer whom Jesus called, and he reinforces this identification by referring to Matthew in the list of the apostles as 'Matthew the publican'. While it could just be an additional piece of factual information, one suspects that something more is at stake, and that this is Matthew's way of emphasizing that the community must have no limits to its membership. Indeed, there is quite a lot of teaching about forgiveness that is unique to Matthew. For example, he alone supplements the Lord's Prayer by adding a comment of Jesus to the effect that there can be no forgiveness unless one forgives in turn (6.14–15). So there is no real conflict with Luke. It is just that concern for the outcast and marginalized is not given as central a place.

So what then is Matthew's central concern, and wherein lies the difference from Luke? It is well encapsulated in the verse that each makes the culmination of a parallel sermon of Jesus. For, if Luke's Sermon on the Plain culminates in the command to 'be merciful, even as your Father is merciful', Matthew's Sermon on the Mount has as its climax to 'be perfect, as your heavenly Father is perfect' (Luke 6.36; Matthew 5.48 RSV).

This call to perfection, the need to 'hunger and thirst after righteousness', is in fact a recurring theme in Matthew's Gospel. What he finds wrong with his fellow-Jews is not their laws, but the fact that they make them finite and *too* easily realizable. In other words, he is worried by any moral code that allows us to rest too easily content with ourselves and so remain unchallenged by the teaching of Jesus. Challenge and unease should be integral to our search for the truth of what is required of us.

Matthew has often been interpreted as calling for a new form of legalism, and there is much in this Gospel which would appear, superficially at least, to support such an interpretation: 'Till heaven and earth pass away, one jot or one tittle shall in no wise pass away from the law' (5.18 AV). Yet that the phrase was original to Jesus seems highly probable in view of the fact that it is also found in Luke (16.17), though he places it in such a throw-away context that it is not at all clear that he had any conception of what Jesus meant. Matthew, however, believes he does, and certainly puts it to highly effective use.

Jesus is portrayed, not as abandoning law, but instead as deepening its significance. A comparison of how Matthew and Mark treat Jesus' attitude to the Sabbath well illustrates the point. Mark's account is very easy to read, with the implication that now no rules whatsoever are to attach to Sabbath observance, whether it be duty to rest or to attend church. To avoid such an interpretation, Matthew omits Jesus' words, 'The sabbath was made for man and not man for the sabbath', and instead supplements Mark's account of Jesus' teaching with additional material in order to show that what Jesus had in mind was not the denial of sabbath obligations, but the insistence that they be set in a wider context in which other obligations and ideals might have to take precedence (cf. Mark 2.23–28 and Matthew 12.1–8). In other words, while a reading of Mark might allow one to think that there might be occasions when one had no obligations, for Matthew what Jesus is saying is that at no point in one's life can one escape the challenge of the gospel: that is, always calling one to do something. Sometimes this is something great, sometimes it is something small, but it is never nothing at all. And that too is why the comment about not a jot or tittle passing from the law is immediately followed by the injunction: 'Except your righteousness shall exceed the righteousness of the scribes and Pharisees, ye shall in no case enter the kingdom of heaven' (5.20 AV).

But are not such standards all too much to bear? No, says Matthew, because such unsettling, apparently impossible, demands are always balanced by the message of forgiveness as proclaimed in the very story that gives the Gospel its name, that of Matthew the publican. So this evangelist at one and the same time challenges us to go beyond whatever point we have reached but also offers us a way out in his message of forgiveness, however far we fall – even to the point of being like that tax-gatherer, a traitor to one's own nation.

So there in a nutshell you have the contrast between the inspiration of the Gospels and so many other perspectives. All three evangelists see clearly that the gospel is there not to endorse, but to challenge themselves and their community. Because they were of very different backgrounds and come from very different communities, the evangelists give very different stresses to their presentation of the gospel. However, that is exactly what we would expect. They could no more escape conditioning by their environment than we can. Where they differ from most of us is not in this respect, but in their ability to answer Christ's summons beyond such conditioning, to hear the gospel not just as an endorsement of themselves, but as a challenge to fresh questions and fresh values. For Mark it constitutes a challenge to all our longings for security; for Luke a summons to look beyond our own comforts and self-identity; for Matthew a law whose demands are infinite. They were willing to press until it hurt. Are we?

20 ❖ The Four Wise Men

—

After his birth astrologers from the east arrived in Jerusalem
(Matt. 2.1 NEB)

Some readers, I suspect, follow their stars – that is to say, they read their horoscopes each morning in the newspaper, to see what the fates have in store for, say, a Libra or a Cancer. (More readers, I suspect, than might be publicly prepared to admit it!) We know that even some popes never acted without consulting their horoscope, one such example being the sixteenth-century Farnese pope, Paul III. But following the stars is of course an even older tradition than that. Astrologers were widely available for consultation throughout the ancient world, whether one looks to Persia, Egypt, or Rome. Just as the moon affects the tide, so it was thought that the coincidence of stars could profoundly affect the nature of a birth, indicating future greatness or even the dawn of a new age. So there is no shortage of accounts in pagan literature of attempts to identify such births, including that of Augustus, the emperor reigning when Jesus was born, and one of his cruel successors, Nero.

In the case of Nero, the word used to describe the astrologers, Magi, is in fact the same word as used in Matthew's Gospel. The Revised Standard Version uses the traditional translation 'wise men', whereas the New English Bible more accurately calls them what Matthew intended: astrologers. For what Matthew's account is concerned to reflect is the way in which the birth of Jesus can answer all those pagan longings for a new age, longings that were so often misdirected. Though his Gospel is often thought to be the most Jewish of the four (and in many ways it is), Matthew's was also equally concerned to assert that, though Judaism gives Jesus' message its firm foundation, it is in fact a gospel for all humankind, and that is why he opens with a Jewish genealogy tracing Jesus' ancestors that includes a number of foreigners such as Tamar, Rahab, and Ruth, and ends with Jesus' injunction to his disciples to make *all* nations his disciples.

The astrologers coming to worship Jesus are thus Matthew's pagan equivalent for all these references to the fulfilment of Old Testament prophecy with which he clutters his Gospel. As the hymn puts it, 'the hopes and fears of *all* the years are met in thee tonight'. It is this truth that we above all need to take on board when thinking about the wise men, and compared to which all other more narrowly historical questions pale into relative insignificance. After all, what does it matter whether there was literally a star that was followed, or whether the wise men behaved more like modern astrologers and consulted their charts? Nor can it have been of much importance to Matthew *who* exactly was there. For he tells us almost nothing about them – just that they were from the east – not even how many of them there were. What matters more for Matthew, and should matter vitally for us, is that Jesus be seen as the fulfilment of *all* pagan hopes (as expressed in all that astrology), whether acknowledged at precisely that moment in history or not.

It is this feature which later versions of the story so brilliantly develop and bring out. Favourite carols such as 'We Three Kings from Orient are' arose because various passages in the Old Testament were thought to refer to Matthew 2, not least Psalm 72.10, which speaks of three kings bearing gifts. Yet even the number three may be a wrong inference. After all, just think how frequently our Christmas stockings are filled with more than one gift from the same person, or Mum and Dad combine to give one large present. However, talk of kings did have at least one enormous advantage: their august state could now nicely balance the shepherds. For in a Christian society there was no longer the same need to emphasize the relevance of the gospel for the pagan, but it was now all the more essential to stress that the privileged and well-to-do kings must kneel before the Christ-Child no less than poor shepherds.

But the Middle Ages went even further. For, though we can now only smile in disbelief when we are told that the three bodies of Melchior, Balthasar, and Caspar were discovered in 1158 and solemnly buried in Cologne Cathedral, we must not forget that their corpses were rightly taken as symbolic of a great and profound truth. One was discovered to be a youth, another middle-aged, and the third an old man, a pattern which was to repeat itself in literally thousands of paintings of the scene, often with one of the kings given black skin, and all with the same end in view: to emphasize the gospel's universal applicability – for all races, all ages, and all ranks of society. All must kneel before God who has become incarnate in this child, if they are to receive healing and peace.

That is why, so far from being embarrassed by these later legendary accretions, I want to glory in them. For they show how deeply the Middle Ages grasped the central Christian message: that Jesus came to meet the needs of us all, rich as well as poor, old as well as young, privileged as well as marginalized. However, perhaps nowhere does this emerge more clearly than in the Russian legend of the fourth wise man. For that fourth wise man could have been any of us, since, like us, he arrives on the scene too late to see the infant child, and so it is with him that I wish to end.

According to one version, he was an Indian prince in search of the perfect recipe for Turkish Delight: that is to say, someone like many of us, already reasonably content with life, but still wanting something more – something that will finally stop that irritating itch of dissatisfaction. Jesus, he hopes, will provide him with the answer, the recipe for perfect contentment as it were, but he keeps narrowly missing an encounter with him, arriving too late even for the Last Supper. However, though – like us – he fails to see Jesus in the Upper Room, he does manage to pick up the leftovers, the crumbs on the table; and as he wets his lips with what remains of the wine, suddenly all is revealed. True contentment comes, as the other three wise men had already discovered decades previously, not through getting but through giving, through, like Christ, giving one's life-blood, dying to self in order that one may be raised to new life. And that was almost certainly Matthew's message too. For, though while we think of the three wise men as wealthy kings the gifts have to be tokens, incense of divinity, gold of majesty and myrrh for burial, if we return to them for one last time as astrologers, what we surely discover is the costliness of the gift to them, gold and expensive perfumes which they could ill afford. But gave they did, and we must too, if we are to receive. To quote one last carol:

> What can I give him
> Poor as I am?
> If I were a shepherd
> I would bring a lamb;
> If I were a wise man
> I would do my part;
> Yet what I can I give him –
> Give my heart.

21 ✤ The Female Revolutionary

—

Then he went home . . . And . . . they went out to seize him, for
they said, 'He is beside himself'

(Mark 3, 19–21 RSV)

Of all the songs that are sung in English parish churches, is there
any which might merit a firing squad? The answer is 'Yes', but to
understand why, and the full significance of that song, we need
first to travel back over the history of our own century.

June 28th, 1994 marked the eightieth anniversary of the fatal
shot that catapulted Europe into the First World War, with the
assassination of the Archduke Franz Ferdinand by a Serbian
nationalist on the streets of Sarajevo. It is one of those facts which
we all learnt at school, but how much easier it is now to comprehend against the background of the terrible destructive forces
that have been unleashed in Bosnia and have torn that country
apart. There is thus a clear sense in which eighty years later we in
Britain understand the strength of nationalistic passions in the
Balkans better than was so at any intervening period.

This is of course a point capable of much wider generaliza-
tion. In 1914, Britain entered the war in a spirit of exuberant
self-confidence, a confidence which was largely shared by the
churches, and was to wreak a terrible havoc on religious belief in
the immediate post-war period. But even in 1919 what happened
in 1914 was still being misperceived as 'the war to end all wars',
and only a tiny minority thought possible what eventually happened, namely another world-wide conflagration a mere twenty
years later. Yet even 1945 was not to yield the full truth about

1914. The depth of nationalistic passions which destroyed three empires in the 1914–18 war runs much deeper than anyone thought, as the nightly bulletins from Sarajevo have made all too clear.

Thus historical events are by no means at their most comprehensible as they happen. Sometimes, generations must pass before a proper understanding at last emerges. In the case of the First World War and that fatal shot at Sarajevo, we are now some eighty years distant, but also in some ways perhaps nearer in comprehension. So too, I suggest, with the Gospels. Anyone reading the synoptic narratives cannot help but be struck by the lack of comprehension by the disciples. Why, for instance, does Peter not discover Jesus' messiahship, far less his divinity, until half way through Mark's Gospel (chapter 8)? As we read, the signs seem obvious, but that is only because we forget that all the Gospels were in fact written with the benefit of hindsight, that is to say, in the light of the resurrection. So, just as a historian writing today about the Archduke's assassination would write with a very different 'feel' from an earlier generation, so all the evangelists write, with the consciousness that all the stumblings of the disciples on the way were of no ultimate significance since the final victory of the resurrection had in fact now been achieved.

Nor is this any different in the case of the birth narratives. The narratives of Matthew and Luke both exude confidence and certainty because both knew how it had all ended. Yet it can hardly have been like that at the time. Mark 3 implies that friends and family alike thought Jesus mad, while John 7 explicitly says that 'even his brothers did not believe in him' (v. 5 RSV). So, even if one of them (James) was to become a leading apostle, and his mother was to be there at the foot of the cross and at Pentecost, I suspect that it was a comprehension slowly and not easily bought. There were just too many ambiguities: rejection in his own native town, hostility from all the leading religious lights, and so forth.

In any case, if it proved hard for all his disciples to understand what Jesus' mission involved, why should this not also have been true of his mother? Any mother would find it difficult to accept her son's abandonment of a secure job for the role of an itinerant preacher. But for Mary it was doubly difficult; her son's conflicts with the Jewish and Roman authorities must soon have given her an inkling of his future death, and for any mother to accept that possibility would have been frighteningly hard: that the body to which she had given birth had now to be broken upon the cross.

But, it may be objected, surely the virginal conception must have made all the difference! Would not so stupendous an event have guarded Mary from all such doubt and uncertainty? At this point, the reader may well expect me to say that the logic of my argument requires denial of the doctrine: that otherwise we generate two contradictory portraits of Mary: the one of the totally assured handmaid of the Lord, the other of a confused girl trying vainly to understand her strange son.

But to suppose that even a virgin birth would speak irrefutably of the hand of God is surely to confuse our own modern certainties with all the misunderstandings of conception which plagued human notions of generation and birth even until relatively modern times. Thus, for example, to the medieval mind unexpected pregnancy conjured up the terror of impregnation by the devil, the so-called incubus, while it was only in 1827, with the discovery of the ovum, that the key role of the woman in conception was at last acknowledged. So for earlier generations the whole notion of pregnancy was infinitely more mysterious and puzzling than it is to us; an inexplicable pregnancy could not thus have the same earth-shattering significance as it would now immediately acquire. But even if for Mary her pregnancy did speak irrefutably of God, there was nothing in Jewish history to suggest that such a pregnancy meant the coming into our world of God himself. Indeed, the whole idea was anathema to the Jewish tradition, with its strict insistence upon an unqualified monotheism. There was thus nothing which could bolster Mary's conviction that here indeed was the hand of God, unlike for us with our two thousand years of Christian history. So all she could do was secretly treasure the knowledge in her heart, perhaps initially too frightened and insecure even to tell her son, in case it fostered his already worrying path towards self-destruction. Only with the resurrection was Jesus vindicated, and perhaps it was only then that Mary finally disclosed her secret.

But, whether so or not, certainly Mary's Song, the Magnificat (Luke 1.46–55), is so unqualifiedly confident that it is hard to conceive of it as anything other than a resurrection song. 'He has filled the hungry with good things and the rich he has sent empty away' would seem to speak of Jesus' ministry rather than of what has just happened to Mary; or again, 'he has put down the mighty from their thrones' surely more naturally speaks of Christ as the exalted Lord now reigning in heaven rather than of Mary's life, which was to remain just as humble and unkingly as before for the next thirty years. And that is in fact what the biblical scholars now tell us: that these are suitable sentiments put into Mary's mouth by Luke in the light of the resurrection rather than her actual words. Indeed, as they stand, they could never have been Mary's actual words, since they make use of the Greek version of the Old Testament and of course Mary would have known no Greek.

When one compares Hannah's Song in 1 Samuel (2.1–10), there would seem little doubt that this provides the conscious model for Mary's Song, and that Luke's narrative is deliberately paralleling Mary's carrying of Jesus with the young Hannah's offer of Samuel to the Lord, just as with the elderly Elizabeth, the Baptist's mother, we are supposed to think of the barren Sarah (Gen. 18.9–14). Indeed, the angelic visitations to Mary (in Luke) and to Joseph (in Matthew) are in all probability also modelled on the Old Testament, where they are also sometimes used to heighten the sense of drama rather than literally record what actually happened.

All these admissions might seem to add strength to the notion of the virgin birth as sheer invention, but it seems to me to give it *greater* conviction. For once the props, as it were, are removed, in come all the ambiguities – a girl convinced that herein lies the hand of God, but not knowing at all precisely what it means. However, we know what it means. For, as with Matthew and Luke, we have the virtue of hindsight. Luke may mention it almost in passing (1.34–35); Matthew offers his usual creative misreading of the Old Testament (1.22–23); but they, like us, know it to declare a wholly new beginning for all humanity, and nowhere is that intended humanity more brilliantly summarized by Luke than in Mary's Magnificat, whatever its ultimate source.

Mary will be called blessed by all generations because it is she who has borne the one who declared by his life and death the overturning of all conventional human values: our respect for the strong and the proud, the mighty and the rich. All come tumbling down with the recognition that God is no respecter of persons, and that the weak and the meek and the lowly are his especial concern, precisely because no one else seems to accord them their proper value. And there at last you have the reason for the firing squad with which we began this chapter – in Nicaragua, whenever the Contras found peasants singing the Magnificat. What they found so objectionable was the peasants' discovery that there was, after all, someone – no less than God himself – who valued those peasants just as they were – hungry, weak, and powerless – and the revolutionary implications that these poor people drew from this.

No doubt some of these peasants behaved in ways that were unchristian, but that should not make us lose sight of the more basic fact that the message of the child Mary carried was, and still is, a revolutionary one. Indeed, dare we say anything else in a world in which millions continue to die of hunger; yet more millions are aborted; tens of thousands are tortured; the mentally handicapped kept firmly out of sight; and where we are constantly told that the only measurement which counts is our achievements, and not simply what we are, frail and vulnerable human beings – vulnerable like the infant coming to birth in Mary's womb? It is that little child that 'puts down the mighty from their seat', and its name? Emmanuel, God with us.

Mary had to struggle towards that conviction, through the confusion of a mysterious birth and the apparently curt dismissal of a wayward son. Yet there she was at the foot of the cross, still longing to comprehend. But comprehend she surely finally did, as the tongues of fire came down on her at Pentecost (Acts 1.14 and 2.1–3). The revolution that she had initiated in bearing her son was now embodied in her very soul. Others wrote the words, but the Magnificant had now become Mary's very own.

22 ❖ Four for the Price of One

—

'Who are you?' He confessed, he did not deny, but confessed, 'I am not the Christ'

(John 1.19–20 RSV)

Were we to give exactly the same sermon text to a number of clergy spread across the length and breadth of the country, it is quite likely that the resultant number of themes would almost exactly match the number of clergy asked! The reason would not be clerical ignorance of Scripture, but the need to address that Scripture to the particular circumstances of their parish – what its pressing problems are, what the congregation heard last week, and so forth. For Christianity is not just about the brute facts of history; it is also about how those facts can relevantly impinge upon our lives in the here and now.

The Gospel writers were faced with exactly the same problem. So for them it is never just a matter of recording events; it is also vitally important to provide a particular perspective on them, one which will challenge and deepen their readers' faith. That is why rediscovering such perspectives can continue to illumine our lives to this today.

Take the case of John the Baptist. That he stood in a special relationship to Christ we now all take for granted. To us, the story of our salvation has a natural, gradual progression as it moves from the Old Testament through the preaching of the Baptist on to Jesus, and then finally into the founding of the Church – and so to ourselves. That is hardly surprising given that there are two thousand years of Christian history and reflection behind us.

117

However, things were very different when the Gospel writers first set to work. They were part of a community that had just experienced God active in an extraordinary way, in the life of Jesus. With his resurrection a new life, a new order, a new community, had been inaugurated, and the Gospel writers' task was to communicate that experience to others. Yet that created a problem for them in how to treat John the Baptist. He was clearly part of the story of Jesus' ministry. Yet the more one said about him, the greater the danger there was of detracting from the unique significance of Jesus. Each of the four evangelists faced that problem, but tackled it in quite different ways. As these continue to have something useful and important to say to us today, I want to look briefly at each in turn.

Mark's Gospel is our oldest. So let us take his account first. Mark is a man in a hurry. He tells the story of Jesus with almost breathless enthusiasm. His narrative races along at break-neck speed, with 'straightway' or 'immediately' often joining incidents together, and so it is not surprising that we find no account of Jesus' birth or childhood. Instead, there is one introductory verse and then we are straight into the voice of John the Baptist crying in the wilderness. Mark's first readers must have been brought up with a start, at the sheer abruptness with which the Baptist suddenly takes the stage, only to lose it within eight verses to Jesus, who also seems to appear, as it were, from nowhere!

This is all part of Mark's technique for making us aware that something radically different, something totally new, is taking place in the history of the world. The Kingdom of God is being brought into existence, and that calls from us, the reader, a total change of heart, a complete turnabout in direction. The Greek for that is *metanoia*, and it is this word that Mark uses to link the message of the Baptist with that of Jesus (1.4, 15). John had already preached that message, but it is Jesus who makes it fully possible in our lives.

St Jerome, the man responsible for the Latin version of the Bible known as the Vulgate, translated *metanoia* by Latin terms from which we derive the two English words 'penitence' and 'penance'. As a result, perhaps inevitably, by the Middle Ages it had commonly come to be glossed as meaning no more than to 'do penance' or 'make amends', and one of the causes of the Reformation was Luther's discovery that *metanoia* meant something much more radical. With the old translation, Luther had agonized over whether he really was doing right by God, whether he really was conquering the old man in him and making sufficient amends, whereas now he saw that that was not the point at all. Rather, it was a matter of God promising the possibility of a totally new start, of a complete turn-around in our lives, regardless of how much of a mess we have made of it up to now. In our present English translations the word 'repent' is used. For us that often connotes purely negative ideas, about regretting the past. Yet while that is important, much more important for Mark is the possibility of this new start that is implied in the Baptist's preaching of repentance, particularly as it is then taken up by Jesus. So much then for Mark.

Matthew and Luke wrote a little later than Mark, and also had additional sources available. While both endorse that call for radical change and a fresh start that we have found in Mark, they also use their additional sources to ensure that this new beginning is not bought at the expense of other things, equally important.

In Luke's case, it is concern that it should not be at the expense of other members of one's society, and to ensure that objective, one finds two elements that are unique to his account. The first is the very precise historical setting that he gives to the Baptist's ministry: 'Now in the fifteenth year of the reign of Tiberius Caesar, Pontius Pilate being governor of Judaea, and Herod being tetrarch of Galilee, and his brother Philip tetrarch of Ituraea and of the region of Trachonitis, and Lysanias the tetrarch of Abilene, Annas and Caiaphas being high priests, the word of God came unto John the son of Zacharias in the wilderness' (3.1–2 AV). This is not just an historical touch (though of course it is that). Rather, Luke's concern is to emphasize that John has *not* come as a bolt out of the blue. There are social reasons why he had to preach at precisely that time and place rather than any other. Thus for Luke it is not an accident that the gospel begins in remote Galilee and then proceeds to Jerusalem and then finally to Rome (at the end of the Acts of the Apostles). It is all part of a great divine plan. But it is a plan in which, though change is required of us, it is not to be a kind in which our social obligations to the particular society in which we are set may be forgotten. So in the second feature unique to Luke, it is he alone of the evangelists who reminds us that John preached, not that tax-collectors for the Empire should give up their jobs, but that they should refrain from extortion, and not that soldiers should leave the Imperial Army in response to the gospel but that they should use force with restraint (3.13–14). So Luke, like Mark, certainly offers us a gospel of change, but unlike Mark he insists that we take our setting in a particular social world with the maximum seriousness.

Matthew is different yet again. Like Luke, he is worried lest this gospel of *metanoia,* of a completely new start, should be misinterpreted. But, whereas with Luke the worry was that this might be taken to imply a neglect of social obligations, Matthew sketches his own distinctive portrait of John to ensure that this should not be at the expense of our debt to the past.

It is well known that Matthew is the most Jewish of the Gospels. For example, he deliberately gathers Jesus' teaching into five blocks of material, so that readers will recall the first five books of the Bible, commonly called in those days the five books of Moses, and then realize that one greater than Moses is here. Again, his Gospel is peppered with Old Testament quotations, pointing the way in which Jesus can be seen as the fulfilment of Israelite religion. However, here I want to draw your attention to just one very minor alteration that Matthew makes to his text.

All the other three Gospels record the Baptist as saying that he is not fit even to 'stoop down and unloose' Jesus' sandal strap, whereas Matthew has the Baptist say that he is not worthy to *carry* Jesus' shoes (Matt. 3.11). Why the difference (surely deliberate, since we know that Matthew had read Mark's Gospel)? Sheer numbers is on the side of the other three Gospels being correct. So what is Matthew up to, in slightly altering the truth of what happened, the truth of what was said?

The point is that to take someone's shoes off was regarded as a very demeaning act in the ancient world, and only a foreign slave was required by law to perform this act. So John, in talking of himself in this way in relation to Jesus, was adopting a position of extreme deference and humility. However, this clearly worried Matthew, in case the point should be misunderstood. What if, he said to himself, my readers draw the conclusion that all God has done before the coming of Jesus is of no importance? What if they fail to give the respect to the Baptist that is his proper due? Thus to avoid any misreading, Matthew modifies just a little what John says so that he can be seen as comparing himself to an unworthy friend (or Jewish slave), and so as not wholly outside the new dispensation, the new order. Of course, nowadays we would add a footnote instead, but that was not the way in the ancient world – there were no such things! So, if the message of the Baptist in Mark is the possibility of a radically new start, and in Luke that this new start should never be at the expense of one's existing social obligations, in the case of Matthew there is added the insistence that all must take place in the context of fully acknowledging our debt to the past, our debt to all the people and events that have made our present lives possible.

And so finally we come to John's Gospel. In some ways this is again more like Mark, with John and Jesus once more suddenly emerging centre-stage. The major difference is that of all the evangelists, John presents the most self-effacing portrait of the Baptist. Most of what he records he shares in common with the other three Gospels, but in his account (John 1.15–34) one thing is unique to him; something made familiar and moving to many of us, thanks to its evocative setting in Orlando Gibbon's anthem 'This is the record of John'. Three times the Baptist is asked 'Are you . . . Elijah, the Messiah, a prophet', and three times he replies: 'I am not'. In recording it thus, John is not just wanting us to think of what the Baptist is not, he is also just as much wanting us to think of who Jesus then is. For seven times later in this Gospel, Christ is recorded as declaring 'I am . . . the Good Shepherd . . . I am the Way, the Truth, and the Life', and so forth, and once simply 'I am'. 'Before Abraham, I am' (8.58), the Christ of John's Gospel declares, thereby identifying himself with the eternal reality of the God once definitely disclosed in Exodus 3 (v. 14).

The threefold 'I am not' is thus John's way of pointing to the 'I am' who is the source of our salvation. But that for John is emphatically not to demote the Baptist's importance. Rather, it is to provide a model for us all as Christians. For, like the Baptist, we too must point away from ourselves to Another; that is what it means to be called Christians. We desire to reflect the love of Christ in our lives, and in so doing to point not to ourselves, but to the Person who makes possible all those occasional flashes of goodness in us.

Four sermons for the price of one. From Mark, the possibility of a new start. From Luke, the need always to take into account our debt to society as it is, warts and all. From Matthew, a reminder of all that we owe to the past. And from John, the perfect portrait of what it is to be a Christian, as one whose life points to another as Saviour and Lord.

23 ❖ The Haemorrhage
of Sin

—

If I only touch his garment, I shall be made well
(Matt. 9.21 RSV)

Many contemporary readers of the Gospels are embarrassed that miracles should feature so prominently. What, however, will undoubtedly surprise them is that this is by no means a modern worry. For if we travel back in time, and examine sermons in the early post-biblical period from the so-called Fathers of the Church, what we in fact discover is a similar embarrassment. Not that they doubted for a moment that miracles had occurred (nor do I), but they did think that nothing very interesting had been said until one went beyond the literal meaning to discern something of relevance to our own lives in the here and now.

Jesus' miracles could of course be used to illustrate the absolute power of God over all his creation, and thereby to underline Jesus' own distinctive status. Such seems to have been the primary intention of Mark: 'Who then is this, that even wind and sea obey him?' (4.41 RSV). However, since for many of the Fathers, for instance John Chrysostom or the early Augustine, miracles had now ceased, to talk of events that now no longer happened was seen as pointless – and indeed, as positively harmful – by raising the wrong type of expectations, much as today we might worry about the false hopes raised in the seriously ill by the sort of charismatic church advertisement that promises miraculous healings at every service.

So, significantly, when Augustine had to preach on the subject of the three occasions when Jesus raises from the dead – Jairus' daughter, the widow of Nain's son, and Lazarus – he quickly passes over the physical side, remarking that death will still come to them in any case, and instead seeks to draw out a spiritual significance, a resurrection of the soul. Let me quote just a few words from one of these sermons. As you will observe, he seeks to make what happened applicable to us all. 'Rise in your heart; go forth from your tomb. For you were lying dead in your heart as in a tomb, and pressed down by the weight of evil habit as by a stone. Now rise and go forth.'

Again, if we take the other miracle with which Matthew intimately links the raising of Jairus' daughter, the healing of the woman with a haemorrhage, a number of the Fathers, St Jerome among them, insist that if the miracle is to be of any permanent significance to us our thoughts should move away from the mere fact of it having happened. In this case because it interrupts the narrative of another and greater miracle, Jerome suggests it may be used to illustrate the way in which God graciously interrupts his purposes for the Jews as the chosen race, in order to deal with us, the Gentiles, and the particular haemorrhage or sin with which we are plagued.

Nowadays, most biblical scholars, and perhaps many readers as well, fight shy of this kind of approach to Jesus' miracles. We tend to think of it as a highly artificial, forced reading of the text. But I'm not so sure; so let me now try to persuade you otherwise.

Admittedly, only John's Gospel tells us that we should interpret Jesus' miracles as signs, but I think that once we start reflecting a little on what life was like in the ancient world and the actual words used in the passage, we shall soon see that both the restoration of life and the deliverance from the haemorrhage could not but be interpreted, even in the first century, as having an essentially spiritual significance, exactly as the Fathers chose to read them.

All three of Jesus' miracles of raising from the dead involve the young: life tragically cut short. What one often forgets is that most life was like that in the ancient world. Accurate statistics are of course impossible for this period, but on the basis of various data one historian has estimated that one in four children in the ancient world died before the age of one, and that even after that initial hurdle was passed, the average life expectancy for a woman was only thirty-four, and for a man forty-six. Now look around you. In the first century AD, the majority of the people you see about you today would already be dead.

A macabre thought, no doubt, but it does help one understand why in the Bible death is seen in such negative terms, and indeed is often, as in Paul, closely associated with sin. For while death will come to most of us as the natural completion of a long and fulfilled life, to the ancient world it came destructively, tragically cutting off the great mass of the human race in their prime – a wasted potential which, like sin, prevented the realization of numerous, positive goods. And so, while we read the three miracles as simply Jesus' kindly response to three sets of mourners – to Jairus, the ruler of the synagogue; to the widow of Nain; and to Martha and Mary, Lazarus' sisters – the ancient world would have seen in these incidents far more: the possibility that humanity's natural condition, its tragic incompleteness, caused just as much by sin's ravages of the soul as death's of the body, could be overcome. So Augustine was surely exactly right: such miracles speak essentially of the overcoming of incompleteness, an incompleteness that is even more pointedly true of our spiritual condition than it is of our physical state.

Let us now return to the woman with a haemorrhage, and reflect for a moment on the condition of those of you who would have still been left alive (assuming the ancient world's life-span) to hear one of the Church Fathers preach in those far off days. If we fall ill in the modern world, almost certainly the cause will be quickly diagnosed; and not only will we know what appropriate steps to take, but should it involve pain, in the vast majority of cases this will be able to be brought under control through various drugs. Now contrast this with the situation in the ancient world. The normal pattern was for illness to strike without any comprehension as to cause or cure, and with no very effective way of controlling pain.

Little wonder then that whereas with us there are many forms of illness that do not stop us enjoying rich and fulfilled lives, disease in the ancient world, even where it did not result in death, was truly devastating. The person needed all their reserves of energy to combat the pain and the uncertainty. So one should not be surprised that disease thus came to function as a natural image for the destructive power of sin: sin when it gains control drains us of all our potential for goodness, just as the woman suffering from the haemorrhage was left with little strength to deal with anything else.

It is the closeness of this parallel that explains one initially rather puzzling feature of the gospel narrative. Most modern versions interpret the woman's words as a simple request for physical healing, and so translate the relevant Greek word as either 'heal', 'cure', or 'make well', whereas in the Authorized Version she asks to be made whole. It is the latter translation which rather nicely captures the ambiguity of the Greek, as the expression used by both her and Jesus is the same word used elsewhere to talk of our salvation. She wants to be saved from her plight and brought to true wholeness of life, and that of course is the desire of all of us, whether we are devastated by an illness or not. We do not want sin and guilt to drain us in the way the woman with the haemorrhage was drained of all her physical powers.

I have spent so long attempting to justify a particular way of reading Jesus' miracles to ensure their continuing relevance that I have left myself with little space to apply the method. Christianity has much to say about how the incompleteness of death may be overcome, but for the moment let us confine ourselves to the image of sin as a haemorrhage. It is of course a strong image, but justified, I believe – most worryingly perhaps, not so much with regard to conspicuous wickedness, as in any sort of situation where a particular fault, not necessarily itself immoral, starts to eat away at the soul: to drain us of our life-blood, and so eventually destroy our whole personality.

HAEMORRHAGE OF SIN

Let me give three brief examples from people I have known, all academics, all distinguished clerics, and all now dead. I think of one who became so obsessed with frustrated ambition that it poisoned every relationship into which he entered, and indeed eventually led to his own death. I think of another whose failure to face his own homosexuality precluded him from an effective ministry because that very failure caused difficulties in his treatment of women. Or I think of a third, whose desperate insecurity led to endless public parading of his achievements; considerable though they were, the net result was that his character was seen by others as simply that of a vain and foolish man.

Three examples chosen at random. Would that such phenomena were rare, but they are not. It can happen even to those who, as in these three cases, are consciously seeking to follow the Christian gospel. So let me end by setting this question squarely before you: Is there a 'haemorrhage' in your own life that needs to be faced, or one which you can help a friend to face? If so, face it sooner rather than later; for only that way can the healing touch of Christ's garment, as in the story, stop the draining of your blood, the draining of your resources for goodness, and bring you back to a full life, restore you to health. There is then a miracle, a miracle that can also be ours.

24 ❖ Blood
at a Wedding

—

On the third day there was a wedding
(John 2.1 NEB)

All of us have, I'm sure, been a guest at a wedding quite a number of times in our lives – and, if you are a cleric like me, it will be many, many times. Each will have been followed by a meal, but there the resemblance ends. With some, the ostentatious desire to impress will have been all too obvious; in others, the desperate attempt to pare down the expense. Some will have ended in a hurried buffet and glass of wine, whereas others continued with dancing throughout the night. Yet in all there would have been present, at least to some degree, the desire to share the joy, to let the love of bride and bridegroom overflow beyond themselves into the larger community, a desire expressed by sharing, sharing in a meal.

But, as I have already hinted, symbol and reality do not always coincide. The bride may hear more from her father about how much it is all costing; or from her mother how they are going to better how Auntie Clare did it for her daughter; or at the service the priest may espy, sitting forlornly at the back, the few who longed to be invited but to whom the invitation never came. And that gap between symbol and reality can of course continue into the marriage. For most of history human sexual love has necessarily had to overflow into others, to be outgoing. Not only were large families an inevitability, there was a social expectation that grandparents also would eventually find a home with the new couple.

Contrast that with today's world, where not merely has the extended family contracted to the atomic, but many couples act almost more like mutual protection agencies, to ward off any wider community. Their homes are never open to a stranger, and when they do emerge into the open air of a new social context, all they do is cling to one another like leeches, so afraid are they of opening themselves to the unknown, to the stranger, to a larger social whole.

This is all very different from first-century Palestine. Even today, Cana is little more than a village, and certainly in that sort of context everybody would have been invited to the wedding – the village idiot just as much as that strange rabbi from Nazareth, only a couple of miles distant.

Now you all think you know what happens next – but do you? The real point has very little to do with Jesus as the generous guest. For in marked contrast to the synoptic Gospels where any notion of miracle as sign is explicitly denied (Mark 8.11–12), in John's Gospel each miracle is recorded as precisely just that: 'This, the first of his signs, Jesus did at Cana in Galilee' (2.11 RSV). John is thus teasing his readers, telling us a story at one level, but constantly hinting that its more profound meaning is to be sought elsewhere. The result is that, when we probe more deeply, what we discover is ourselves as the guests, and Christ as the bridegroom.

In some of the most beautiful and moving passages of the Old Testament, God had been described as Israel's bridegroom, as the lover whom his people had spurned, and it is an image which we find Jesus in the synoptic Gospels taking to himself as God's representative; for instance, Mark 2.19: 'Can the wedding guests fast while the bridegroom is with them?' (RSV). So now, in this passage, John intends us to identify Jesus as the bridegroom at his own wedding feast, disclosing what true love, a true marriage, is like: one in which we become wholly identified with him, wholly in love with him and he with us, but in an outgoing, not a self-seeking, protective love.

Yet when asked to turn water into wine, note his words to his mother: 'My hour has not yet come'. Once more John is offering us a code, a pointer or reminder to the reader of a deeper significance, with the allusion to a yet more famous and terrible occasion when those same words were once more uttered, in Jesus' final prayer before he goes to his death: 'Father, the hour has come' (17.1 RSV). Indeed, just in case you miss the connection, over the intervening chapters John repeats the theme of the hour not yet come no less than half a dozen times. So we are also expected to think of Jesus' death, yet equally of his resurrection: 'on the *third* day there was a marriage'. For John, death and resurrection are but one; they speak a single message, and that perhaps goes some way towards explaining how marriage can here also be treated as a death: a true marriage comes through a dying to self.

However, before we focus more narrowly on what could conceivably be meant by that, observe one further detail of the more positive imagery: the six large stone jars, normally used for Jewish rites of purification. Six, one less than the traditional biblical perfect number of seven; in other words, the Old Testament had its place, but it is about to yield to something altogether more wonderful. The everyday water becomes wine, the sign of celebration, the sign of community; drunk among Jews, as with us, only on special social occasions. Not just wine, though, but wine in abundance, wine overflowing – no less than one hundred and twenty gallons of it! Everyone can become part of this party; everyone is a wedding guest when Jesus is the bridegroom.

But then comes the rub. For, remembering the double reading, the wine turns into blood, the symbol of Christ's death. Communal celebration, the community going beyond oneself, has its cost. T. S. Eliot once described the Eucharist in horrifyingly stark language as 'the dripping blood our only drink, the bloody flesh our only food'. Yet for all its starkness, his image contains a profound truth. For there really can be no marriage without that 'for worse', no son or daughter without the disappointment of rejection or rebellion, no friend who never lets you down, no community to which you belong which never betrays its ideals – in short, no resurrection without death. Pain and hurt are there in all human relationships; nevertheless, it is only by opening ourselves up to such hurt that we can then gain the capacity to transform those relationships into something deeper.

All his disciples failed Jesus. On the cross, it seemed as if even his Father had betrayed him. Yet Jesus remained open to others, open to the centurion at the foot of the cross, open to the thieves dying with him, and ultimately open to that same Father who had seemingly betrayed him: 'Father, into your hands I commit my spirit' (Luke 23.46 JB).

And the result? The blood poured from his side into the chalice on the altar. The possibility of real marriage, real friendship, real community, opened up. It liberated those first disciples, and it can still liberate us. As our society everywhere disintegrates into possessive individualism, the blood flowing on the altar tells a very different tale: of a costly marriage feast in which all are loved, all cared for, with the blood strangely tasting as refreshing and liberating as wine.

25 ✤ In Praise
of Hypocrisy

—

Unless your righteousness exceeds that of the scribes and
Pharisees, you will never enter the kingdom of heaven
(Matt. 5.20 RSV)

John Major's decision to launch a 'Back to Basics' policy was
much criticized. The rightness or wrongness of that policy I do
not wish to consider, but one feature of the debate which did
puzzle me was the all but universal assumption that hypocrisy is a
wholly bad thing. That seems to me far from obvious. So what I
would like to explore here is the possibility that a society in which
hypocrisy is present is in fact, however paradoxical it may seem,
immeasurably superior to a society without it. In the process what
I hope we shall also discover is something about the nature of
Jesus' principal opponents, the Pharisees: why it was that, despite
the severity of some of Jesus' judgements upon them as hypocrites, he could none the less also admire them, and even hold
them as a model which our own standards must surpass.

Opposed to my assessment of hypocrisy may be set the oft
heard claim that our own society is indubitably superior to the
Victorian age, riddled as it undoubtedly was with hypocrisy. But I
seriously doubt whether we are really entitled to indulge in such
self-satisfied congratulations. Let me explain.

For a start, it should be remembered that the Victorians themselves were fully aware of the hypocrisy inherent in their society. It
thus is in no way a discovery of the twentieth century: it was
something the nineteenth century already knew for itself. Consider, for instance, this brilliant parody by the poet, Arthur Hugh

Clough, of the way in which fellow-Victorians treated the Ten Commandments:

> ·Thou shalt have one God only; who
> Would be at the expense of two?
> No graven images may be
> Worshipped except the currency:
> Swear not at all, for, for thy curse
> Thine enemy is none the worse:
> At church on Sunday to attend
> Will serve to keep the world thy friend:
> Honour thy parents; that is, all
> From whom advancement may befall:
> Thou shalt not kill: but needst not strive
> Officiously to keep alive:
> Do not adultery commit;
> Advantage rarely comes of it:
> Thou shalt not steal; an empty feat
> When it's so lucrative to cheat.
> Bear not false witness; let not the lie
> Have time on its own wings to fly:
> Thou shalt not covet, but tradition
> Approves of all forms of competition.

And then, just in case the Christian thinks that he has escaped – with the poem so far having been based exclusively on the Ten Commandments – Clough adds the following scathing criticism of attitudes towards Christ's Summary of the Law:

> The sum of all is, thou shalt love,
> If anybody, God above:
> At any rate shall never labour
> MORE than thyself to love thy neighbour.

But, you may say, so what? All I have so far shown is that the Victorians were, after all, conscious of the hypocrisy that was endemic to their society, not that the presence of such hypocrisy was in any sense a good thing. True; but let us now go on to ask why hypocrisy was then present to such a degree, but so largely absent today.

Certainly it has something to do with our own world being more open and more honest, and that is good. However, I am convinced that it also has a lot to do with something much less commendable, that is to say, with the collapse of ideals, and their replacement with something more trivial but easier to implement: a set of easily realizable moral ends. For what produces hypocrisy? Is it not the tension between ideal and reality, the tension between the conviction that one ought to be achieving something better and the realization that one has in fact fallen far short? Hypocrisy then arises as a form of insulation or protection, as a means of disguising the truth from oneself, the truth one finds too hard to bear, of the gap between ideal and reality. Instead, one pretends; one acts out the part (the literal meaning of the word 'hypocrite'), as though the ideal had in fact been realized.

That said, there would now seem an obvious explanation of why hypocrisy is largely absent from our own age, yet was so deeply rooted in the Victorian. For it is surely impossible to deny that Victorian society was a society of ideals, whereas our own is basically a cult of mediocrity, and that is as true of morality as of anything else. Modern England is just not the sort of society to produce the characteristic tension between ideal and reality that was endemic to Victorian England.

The contrast emerges in numerous ways. Think, for instance, of buildings. For the Victorians, a railway station was an expression of social purpose and order; for us, it is merely a work of utility. The same contrast even applies to church buildings. Victorian Gothic aspires loftily to the skies; the typical modern church squats embarrassingly, trying not to draw too much attention to itself. Or think of the National Theatre in London. From the point of view of putting on a dramatic production, it serves its purpose admirably, but, like the rest of the South Bank complex, on the outside it says nothing about the power of drama to uplift the human spirit, so powerfully declared in many a Victorian theatre.

With morality, the contrast is even more effectively made. For what was a parody in Clough is now argued as the basis for social action – as with one Oxford philosophy don, who in all innocence used Clough's words ('Thou shalt not kill: but needst not strive officiously to keep alive') as a motto for his own defence of abortion and euthanasia. The parody has become the reality. The tension of the ideal has gone, and with it any temptation towards hypocrisy. But at what price?

Contrast now our own age with Jesus' situation in first-century Palestine. He was addressing a society that was in many ways more like Victorian society than our own – a society riddled with hypocrisy but also riddled with ideals. Some of Jesus' most severe comments are reserved for the Pharisees: 'Woe unto you, scribes and Pharisees, hypocrites!' (Matt. 23.13 AV). Yet no one can read the Pharisaic literature of the time without coming away deeply impressed by their tremendous ·idealism and the seriousness with which they took moral issues. Even all that ritual cleansing seems to have had a laudable purpose: the attempt to make all life holy, the home no less than the Temple. Of course, the resulting tension between idealism and reality no doubt sometimes generated hypocrisy, the merely acting out of a part, but one is certainly not entitled to conclude from the Gospels that as a breed they all behaved thus. In fact, we find some – like Nicodemus – searching Jesus out (John 3), while even the Pharisee whose prayers are condemned in comparison with those of the publican was by implication a better human being than most of us (Luke 18.11–12). He is never dishonest, tithes all he has, fasts twice a week, and so on.

What Jesus attacks is not his ideals, but his self-righteousness about them. Even so, if anything, Jesus makes the tension with ideals even more unmanageable. Thus in the Sermon on the Mount we learn that not merely is killing wrong, but even being angry with your brother in your heart; not just adultery, but any thought of lust at all; not merely false swearing, but any telling of lies that makes oath-taking necessary as a guarantee of the truth, and so on – all summed up in that impossibly high demand: 'You, therefore, must be perfect, as your heavenly Father is perfect' (Matt. 5.48 RSV).

Our Lord thus built tension between ideal and reality into the very heart of his ethical message; and with that, inevitably, also the temptation towards hypocrisy. For, though 'with God all things are possible' (Matt. 19.26 RSV), very few of us are likely to get even remotely near to that ideal, and so the temptation is either to abandon the faith and adopt the mediocrity of modernity, or else turn to some form of self-deceiving hypocrisy.

But Christ was of course wiser than all our follies, and where his uniqueness lies is in offering a clear way out of that tension that keeps the ideal still firmly in focus. What he suggests is that the attempt to live up to the ideal is sustainable only if we have constantly before our eyes the image of divine forgiveness, requested daily in the Lord's Prayer, itself part of the Sermon on the Mount: 'Forgive us our trespasses'. The image of the Father running to meet the Prodigal Son is an image which suggests that it is not at all for us to judge how far we have progressed along the road, not at all for us to worry about the gap between ideal and reality. We are certain to fail again and again, but on each occasion of failure God is always there, more than willing to meet us and to offer his aid, so that we can start afresh.

The tension thus dissolves in the loving care of God. The tragedy is that the hypocrite cannot see this. He thinks either that everything depends on his own efforts, or that success is the only measure of worth, and thus he tries to disguise his failures in a life of pretence.

In conclusion, then, when next you encounter hypocrisy either in yourself or in others, do not necessarily despise it. For it may well be a good sign, of a longing for more than mediocrity, and more than mediocrity is what both Church and nation alike desperately need.

26 ✣ The Scribe in Need of Forgiveness

—

Father, forgive them; for they know not what they do
(Luke 23.34 RSV)

I began my undergraduate career as a classicist, and I well remember the irritation with which I heard lecture after lecture on textual variants and how we might choose between them. To this day, I still think that we should have spent more time on considering the themes of the plays themselves, on what makes Greek drama such profound and moving literature. However, with the passing of the years I have also grown a little wiser: variant readings can after all sometimes greatly alter the meaning of a text as a whole; and, even where that is not so, can still cast interesting light on how the scribe himself understood the text. My focus in what follows will be upon the psychology of one particular biblical scribe, one particular person who helped to pass on to us the text that we have today. But first let me set him in the wider context of the history of the transmission of the biblical text as a whole.

In marked contrast to other works from the ancient world, the biblical scholar has in fact a wealth of early manuscript traditions upon which to draw. But that far from disposes of all problems. For occasionally the disagreements are significant, and so much, as in the classical case, may hang on the choice of a particular reading. For instance, if we take the Old Testament, it used to be thought that its Hebrew manuscripts were closer to the original than the Greek translation made in the third century BC, known as the Septuagint, and that our difficulties in comprehending what could be meant were simply the result of inadequate knowledge of early Hebrew. However, the discovery of the Dead Sea Scrolls in 1947 at Qumran disclosed that the Septuagint is in fact based on a different, and often more easily intelligible, Hebrew text, and that is why in modern Bibles you will often find a footnote indicating that the Greek reading has now been preferred to the Hebrew.

In the New Testament there have been fewer changes, but every now and then they can be quite significant. For example, in the Authorized Version you will find a rather fine evocation of the Trinity in 1 John 5.7, but unfortunately in modern versions this has had to go since it was clearly an improvement made to the text by a scribe who thought the author's reference to three earthly witnesses – spirit, water, and blood – could be balanced nicely by the heavenly triad – Father, Son, and Holy Spirit. That omission seems to me a loss, but equally there can be gains. Take chapter 4 of the same epistle. The Authorized Version has 'we love him, because he first loved us' in verse 19, whereas modern versions omit the pronoun and so have 'we love because he first loved us'. Instead of John merely talking about a *quid pro quo*, that we decide to love God because he first did something for us, we now have the much more profound thought, that all our loves, for our fellow human beings as much as for God, stem and flow from the love at the very centre of the universe, the love that lies in the very heart of God.

And so at last I come to my scribe, and the text of John 7.53–8.11, the story of the woman taken in adultery. So overwhelming is the manuscript tradition against this being originally part of John's Gospel that many modern versions, the New English Bible included, print it as an appendix. The style and vocabulary are in any case very unlike the rest of this Gospel. It is closest to that of Luke, which presents an interesting irony. For another famous passage about forgiveness (which also has its textual problems) occurs in Luke, Jesus' cry from the cross: 'Father, forgive them; for they know not what they do' (23.34). It is omitted in two of our best manuscripts, the Codex Vaticanus and the Codex Bezae.

What could have happened? Presumably in the latter case the scribe copying Luke just could not bring himself to believe that God had forgiven so heinous a crime. After all, the Jews as God's chosen people ought to have recognized the presence of the Messiah in their midst, the man who was intended to be the culmination of all their history. Indeed, the scribe might have argued, was it not clear that God had not forgiven them, since Jerusalem was devastated in AD 70, and all Jews permanently expelled from the city in 135, when it was renamed Aelia Capitolina? But he was of course wrong. Jesus had spoken of forgiving 'unto seventy times seven', that is, without limit, and from where else could Stephen have learnt to forgive, even as he was being stoned than from the example of his Lord?

In the case of the story of the woman taken in adultery, it is no longer possible to identify for certain where in Luke's Gospel it might once have occurred. There is some manuscript evidence to suggest that it once had its place at Luke 21.38, just before the narrative of the preparation for the Last Supper. Yet, whatever the truth of this, that it represents a genuine incident from Jesus' life, there would seem little doubt. Allusion is made to it by a number of ancient writers, including for example the author of the *Apostolic Constitutions* and Eusebius. So why omit the incident? In all probability, here once again we have a case of a scribe doubting the range of God's forgiveness: could it *really* extend to someone responsible for the break-up of a marriage? Indeed, we find just such an attitude reflected in the early discipline of the Church, for along with murder and apostasy, adultery was regarded so seriously as to be seen as incapable of forgiveness after baptism – which is why baptisms were often delayed, the Emperor Constantine's among them.

Today, of course, we live in a very different world. We are all too aware of how external pressures such as upbringing and environment can affect the likelihood of one committing a crime, or how traumatic internal pressures may be within a marriage. The result is that the notion of forgiveness without limit comes easily to us, and from that it is but a short step to viewing the scribe who made these changes with contempt, as someone who – unlike us – failed to take Jesus' teaching on forgiveness with sufficient seriousness. But is that really fair? Has perhaps the modern world not also neglected important aspects of Jesus' teaching, in particular the whole question of the cost of forgiveness?

Take first the question of crime, crimes like those of the penitent thief. So used are we to identifying external causes for crime, that we forget that nothing can be done to transform the criminal until he has first admitted that he has done something wrong. While an ordinand, the Home Office allowed me to spend a fortnight as a prisoner, and certainly the most fascinating discovery which I made during that time was that practically everyone in prison believes that they are innocent – not in the sense that they do not admit to having done the deed, but that they deny its seriousness. So, for instance, those in prison for embezzlement would argue that everyone fiddles their income tax anyway; those in for theft would point out that at least they didn't use violence; those in for violent crimes, that at least they weren't rapists; rapists, that at least it wasn't little children, and in any case she was 'asking for it any way', and so on. Yet without a costly facing up to one's past and a recognition that one's present punishment is deserved, how will it be possible for the future ever to be truly transformed? Contrast, then, the words of the penitent thief to his fellow on the cross: 'In our case we deserved it; we are paying for what we did' (Luke 23.41 JB). It is surely that admission which enabled Jesus to foresee his transformation, and so promise: 'Today shalt thou be with me in paradise' (Luke 23.43 AV).

Again, if one turns now to think of adultery, it is easy to slide from the admission that in many, perhaps most, cases no single party is entirely to blame to the claim that no one really deserves blame. So the talk becomes all about 'irretrievable breakdown', and no serious attempt is made to face the faults that have resulted in the present situation and the sad consequences which often accrue from them, such as insecure children. Yet, once more, unless that costly effort is made to face one's past, the character defects which led to the first breakdown will still be present when a second marriage is attempted – something which is surely confirmed by statistics, which reveal that second marriages are in fact more likely to break down than first – almost exactly a half.

The ancient world in which a scribe found it impossible to believe in the boundless character of divine forgiveness; the modern world in which we find it hard to accept its costly character. Can either world really afford to stand in judgement on the other? Do we not need corrections to both: to the modern world that without that costly facing of ourselves, even God remains powerless to act; and to the ancient, that once we have so opened ourselves to God, then our past, however awful (though never obliterated), can indeed be wonderfully transformed into God's own glorious future?

So, textual criticism not only has its uses, but also its lessons!

27 ✤ Wanting
It All to End

—

But in those days, after that tribulation, the sun shall be darkened,
and the moon shall not give her light'

(Mark 13.24 AV)

When asked to think of a synopsis, most readers, I suspect, will call to mind those nasty little exercises we all had to do at school as part of English comprehension. You know the sort of thing – trying to produce a précis of what already seems an all too dense a passage. For biblical scholars, however, a synopsis means something altogether different: it is a book set out in parallel columns, allowing direct and immediate comparison of how each of the Gospel writers records a specific event or speech. Sometimes the results are fascinating, and what Mark and Luke make of the tribulations that are to befall Jerusalem (Mark 13; Luke 21.5–36) is one such case in point.

Tradition has it that the young man who fled naked from the garden of Gethsemane (Mark 14.51–52) was Mark himself. True or not, this well conjures up the spirit of his Gospel: of a young man in a rush, not now to escape arrest, but to win others for Christ. There is no careful introduction as in Matthew's and Luke's Gospel. Instead, we are immediately thrown into the thick of things, with John the Baptist's call to repentance, and a sort of urgent staccato is then maintained throughout the narrative, particularly by repeated use of the word 'immediately' to connect one incident with the next. It is an urgency that is further reinforced by a sense of mystery. Not only does his Gospel begin by throwing us *in medias res* without explanation, originally it also ended on the same note at

16.8, with the tomb empty, but Jesus not yet seen and the disciples 'afraid' – the very last word of his text. In other words, we are constantly being pressurized by Mark into asking: Who is this strange man, who has command of wind and water, and promises us health and wholeness? – a pressure that Mark believes calls for immediate decision, for conversion to Christ.

It is against this background that I think we must read his account of Jesus' mysterious words about what is to provoke Jerusalem's sad fate. Whereas Matthew helpfully tells us from where this strange phrase 'the abomination of desolation' comes – the Book of Daniel – Mark is deliberately allusive, in order to force us to reflect further. From its original context we know that what was meant was an act of desecration to the Temple. Elsewhere in the Gospel, Jesus speaks of its forthcoming destruction, as well as in more general terms of the fate of Jerusalem. Nor were such comments really surprising. Given the strength of nationalistic fervour, to any neutral observer it must have looked well nigh certain that sooner or later an explosion would occur, wreaking havoc for the future life of the nation.

What is surprising, though, is Mark's linking of such comments with the expectation of the end of the world, as is obvious from the immediately following verses where the connecting phrase 'in those days' (vs. 19.24) seems clearly to imply no significant time-gap between the two events. So from Jerusalem's fall we seem to move inevitably towards the sun being darkened, and stars falling from heaven, and the Son of Man coming in clouds of glory. My suspicion is that, so keen is Mark to press home his call for immediate decision, the call to conversion, that he has combined two sets of sayings of Jesus about the future of the nation and the fate of the world, sayings that were once quite distinct. After all, it is a much more effective preaching ploy to say not just 'decide before our nation is destroyed', but 'decide before the world ends, and that is coming soon'. Another factor may also have been strongly imminentist expectations in the air, such as we find in the earlier writings of Paul (e.g. 1 Cor. 7.29). Given the overwhelming character of the early disciples' experience of the resurrection, it was perhaps inevitable that many in the community came to expect that a new age was just about to dawn.

However that may be, the destruction of the Temple did indeed come in AD 70, and Daniel's words thus found their proper application, with Titus' army of destruction setting up its standards in the Temple, offering pagan sacrifices within its very walls, and carrying off its treasures, before finally razing the building to the ground. Luke, unlike Mark, not only writes after these tragic events, but realizes that if the Church's mission is to succeed, it must now finally break free of Mark's obsession with the end of the world, and instead come to terms with the greatest power within it: Rome. So, first he rewrites Mark's mysterious allusion in order to make clear that this has already happened. So Luke's version reads 'when you see Jerusalem surrounded by armies, then know that its desolation has come near' (21.20 RSV). More importantly, he warns the reader against thinking that this has anything to do with the end of the world. For inserted between the two blocks of material is now the qualification that 'Jerusalem shall be trodden down of the Gentiles, until the times of the Gentiles be fulfilled' (Luke 21.24 AV). In other words, there are to be centuries in between. And in the meantime, Luke is adamant that the Church's strategy must be more than simply a demand for personal conversion; rather, it must see the whole Gentile world and its institutions as its own proper inheritance, and that is why Luke ends part two of his Gospel, the Acts of the Apostles, in the very heart of the Empire, in Rome itself. Indeed, so concerned is Luke to undermine his fellow-Christians' hostility to the Empire that he offers us a very sympathetic portrait of Pilate, and even omits the bad treatment of Jesus at the hands of the Roman soldiers.

But what, then, of ourselves? What can these two very different portrayals of Jesus' message have to say to us today?

Almost all British institutions are currently under a cloud, whether one thinks of the monarchy, police, judges, politicians, or even the Church itself. Under such circumstances it would be very easy for us to try to retreat either into cynicism or into a holy ghetto. But if Luke could *dare* to see the Church's future as the leaven in the lump, permeating as cruel an empire as Rome's, can we as his successors in the faith dare any less? Of course, the world is an ambiguous place, but the way to change, to transform it, is to engage at every level with it, even if at times that means partaking of all its ambiguities. Yet equally that cannot be the whole Christian answer. For we would certainly be overwhelmed by these same ambiguities unless at our centre there also beats the converted heart of which Mark speaks. Christianity is thus equally a summons to immediate personal change, a summons to be different.

And what, finally, of the point over which Mark erred? With the possibility of a nuclear holocaust around the corner, some of you well may wish to share his pessimism about the imminence of the world's end. But, whether so or not, what we can all surely appropriate is Jesus' teaching that as individuals we must always live in the light of our death, that we never know when it will be said to us: 'This night your soul is required of you' (Luke 12.20 RSV). That emphatically does not mean that we should be for ever thinking about our death, but it does mean that we should be for ever thinking about the gospel of love to which we are called, about whether this and every night we shall fall asleep, leaving the world a better place.

The novelist Thornton Wilder expresses it far better than I ever could. So let me end with the famous conclusion to his novel *The Bridge of San Luis Rey*: 'Soon we shall die . . . and we ourselves shall be loved for a while and then forgotten. But the love will have been enough; all those impulses of love return to the love that made them. Even memory is not necessary for love. There is a land of the living and a land of the dead, and the bridge is love, the only survival, the only meaning.'

28 ❖ The Alternative Eucharist

—

'Then, Lord . . . not only my feet, but my hands and my head
as well'

(John 13.9 JB)

Anyone who takes the time to sit down and read straight through
one of the Gospels at a single sitting and reflects which of their
favourite stories have occurred and which have not, cannot help
but be startled by some of the discoveries they make. For instance,
unique to Luke are many of the incidents concerned with women
or outcasts – the widow of Nain and the woman who was a sinner
in chapter 7, or the story of the Prodigal Son in chapter 15, or the
parable of the rich man and poor beggar at his gate in chapter 16,
and so on.

Again, with the Gospel of John there are quite a few surprises,
not least the fact that in his account, while Jesus washes his
disciples' feet at the Last Supper, there is, unlike the other three
evangelists, no record of him instituting Holy Communion. This
has led some New Testament scholars, for instance the distinguished German theologian Rudolph Bultmann, to claim that
John was really anti-sacramental, and that in consequence even
passages which sound deeply sacramental such as John 6 –
'unless you eat the flesh of the Son of Man and drink his blood,
you have no life in you' (v. 53 RSV) – cannot possibly be original
to the text.

That is not something which I believe, but in order to see what
a more likely explanation is, both of John 6 and this strange
omission, it is necessary to take seriously something we do not

always regard with sufficient seriousness, namely symbolism and its relation to action.

Let us begin by recalling the practice of sacrifice in the Old Testament. The two most common types were burnt sacrifices and peace-offerings. With the former, as the name implies, everything was burnt, whereas with the latter, as Leviticus 3 records, the blood was drained off and then poured out on the ground or sprinkled on the altar, while the worshipper and the priest ate the flesh of the animal concerned. Now the point of going through the ritual was of course to symbolize something. First, the blood was regarded as the life of the animal; and because all life was seen as belonging to God, what the worshipper acknowledged in *not* consuming the blood was that the power of life and death belonged not to himself but to God alone as creator; and that is the reason why the blood would be sprinkled on the altar, the altar being seen as expressive of what properly belongs to God. But, secondly, at the same time the worshipper consumed the flesh, thereby symbolizing that his life and God's were none the less bound up as one, through sharing in the same animal. They were at peace with one another through sharing a common meal.

The Prayer Book defines a sacrament as 'an outward and visible sign of an inward and spiritual grace', and of course this is exactly what this peace-offering was intended to be – an outward act, an outward symbol of an inward transformation – with the individual now resolving to live in such a way that he could be at peace with God.

However, as the prophets saw clearly, the problem with symbols is that they can very easily be treated as the reality itself, and that was a corruption that seems to have happened all too frequently in ancient Israel. The rituals were gone through, without any thought of inward transformation. Recall, for instance, Hosea's frequent condemnations: 'I desired mercy, and not sacrifice; and the knowledge of God more than burnt offerings' (6.6 AV).

Yet if the prophets say that, Jesus saw it even more clearly – but also the way in which the meaning of the symbolism of sacraments could be made forever real for us. At the first Passover, as described in Exodus 12, there had been the same division of flesh and blood as in the peace-offering – blood on the door lintels, you will remember, and a Passover lamb hurriedly eaten before the Israelites fled from Egypt. But now Jesus at the Last Supper, itself a Passover meal, identifies the eating of the flesh, the sign of peace with God, with his own approaching sacrifice on the cross: 'This is my body which is given for you'. The symbolism of the sacrament could scarcely be more explicit. Reconciliation with God, the peace that the peace-offering was intended to effect, the deliverance that eating the Passover lamb was intended to bring, demands not just a ritual act, the eating of flesh, but the offering of our very selves, just as Christ was about to offer himself on the cross for his disciples and for us.

Not only that, though. Jesus goes one stage further; he invites us to share in the *blood* of the offering as well. Now, at one level this simply refers to the complete offering of Jesus, 'flesh and blood' being a common way in the Bible of referring to the complete person. But, given the sacrificial context with all the traditional associations of what was supposed to happen to the blood, it could not be otherwise than that the disciples must have experienced a profound shock at what Jesus was doing. For as I have already noted, the blood was seen as the essential life force, and thus as belonging exclusively to God.

Indeed, we know that, because of this, drinking of blood was regarded with peculiar horror, as a usurpation of the divine prerogative, the divine power over life and death. There are numerous passages you could look up, but let me just mention one – Leviticus 17.10: 'Whatsoever man. there be of the house of Israel . . . that eateth any manner of blood; I will even set my face against that soul . . . and will cut him off from among his people' (AV).

So Jesus, in suggesting that his sacramental peace-offering does involve the consumption of blood, could not help but cause shock and consternation among his disciples, who must only have gradually realized what he meant – that Jesus through his death was pointing not just the way towards sacrificial reconciliation with God (vital though that is), but also now offering to his disciples and to all of us a share in that *divine* life, as symbolized in the blood – an eternal life that knows no end.

None of this is mentioned in the Synoptic Gospel's account of the institution of the Eucharist, but it is all brilliantly brought out by John in that beautiful meditative chapter 6. Three times he makes the connection between the sacrament and eternal life, the life that can now be ours through participation in, and identification with, that first sacrifice of Christ's. We are told that unless we drink this blood, there can be no life in us, while we are also promised that 'whoever eats my flesh and drinks my blood possesses eternal life, and I will raise him up on the last day' (John 6.54 NEB).

But, if that explains the significance of the language there, the preference for the talk of flesh and blood rather than body and blood, and the intimate connection with eternal life, what of John's omission of the narrative of the institution of Communion at the Last Supper?

Throughout what I have said so far I have been highlighting the inherent problem of all sacramental action – that the symbol can get divorced from the reality – and the way in which Jesus, by making the sacrament of our peace with God more directly connected with his own personal sacrifice, tried to overcome this problem. However, as Christians we are well aware that such a divorce between the two, between the ritual and the intention, can happen *even* in the Eucharist. We approach Communion without any proper preparation and without any real intention of offering ourselves in the way Christ offered himself to the Father. My suspicion is that by the time John wrote his Gospel, the last of the four, written about AD 95, this was already becoming a problem in the Church. And what John does is offer a very imaginative solution.

His Gospel is full of symbolism. So, for example, the first miracle he records is that at Cana of Galilee, and thereby, we are forcibly reminded that Jesus is here to bring new life – no mere water, but wine in abundance. Again, unlike the Synoptics, he opens Jesus' ministry with an account of the cleansing of the Temple, and so right from the start we are reminded that Jesus is author of a new order, a new dispensation. Therefore, throughout his Gospel one is expecting to perceive deeper significance than the mere surface meaning of the text.

So what happens to the reader when he or she comes to chapter 13 and the Last Supper is mentioned? One is immediately brought up with a jolt. For, where one would have expected to read the words of institution, there is silence, not a whisper. But that is not to say that there is nothing at all. Instead, we have Jesus washing his disciples' feet, Peter's initial refusal, then Jesus' comment: 'If I do not wash you, you can have nothing in common with me', and Peter's impetuous response: 'Then, Lord, not only my feet, but my hands and my head as well' (John 13.8–9 JB). And the whole narrative culminates with Jesus' comment: 'Do you understand what I have done to you? You call me Master and Lord and rightly; so I am. If I, then, your Lord and Master, have washed your feet, you should wash each other's feet' (13.13–14 JB).

Given so much use of symbolism elsewhere in John's Gospel, what I think he is doing here is powerfully reminding the reader of what the symbolic action of Communion is really all about. His readers, like you and I, already know the words of institution, but we can so easily let them pass into empty ritual, into a mere form of words. So John pulls us up with a start, and records at the very point at which we are expecting the institution of the Eucharist what the outward and visible sign of this sacrament is inwardly pointing to: the complete transformation of our lives into Christ's likeness – our readiness to serve as he served, to love as he loved, to sacrifice ourselves for others as he gave himself first for us.

Then, Lord, not just my feet, but my hands and my head also.

29 ❖ Wrestling in Prayer

—

And being in an agony he prayed more earnestly; and his sweat was
as it were great drops of blood

(Luke 22.44 AV)

My theme here will be the danger of sanitizing our prayers, of
assuming that we must be in a fit state before we can even begin to
pray; the danger of assuming that we can only present, as it were,
our best side to God. The consequence of this is that we often try
to resolve our tensions and worries *before* we kneel to ask for God's
aid in bringing acceptance of his will for us. The trouble with such
a concept of prayer is, of course, that the most crucial stage in
coming to such acceptance – the agonizing, the indecision, the
struggling with the worse side of ourselves – is placed firmly outside the divine orbit, and it is little wonder then that people come
to doubt even the value of prayer itself. For on this understanding, instead of being at the heart of our decision-making pro-
cedures it has become, as it were, merely the icing on the cake:
the saying of 'fiat' (let thy will be done) to what has effectively
already been decided.

To conceive of prayer in this way is no mere modern temptation. The two types of attitude to prayer are in fact to be found
within the Bible itself, and may be well illustrated by considering
two very different versions of the story of Jesus' agony in the
Garden of Gethsemane, as they are presented by Mark and Luke.
Was Jesus' prayer in Gethsemane a real struggling, a real wrestling
with himself and what might or might not be the divine will for
him, or does his prayer instead constitute a fairly calm acceptance

151

of what he has already clearly seen to be demanded of him? 'Father, if thou art willing, remove this cup from me; nevertheless not my will, but thine, be done' (Luke 22.42 RSV). Were we to look to these words alone (common to both Mark and Luke), Jesus' prayer would seem perhaps more naturally to suggest the latter interpretation, and indeed in subsequent Christian history that is how they have often been used: as a model of prayer not as struggle or conflict, but as calm acceptance of the divine will, whatever it may bring.

Yet, once we turn to an examination of the description of the incident as a whole (Mark 14.32–42; Luke 22.39–46), a very different picture emerges. What we in fact find is a fascinating to and fro between these very different approaches to what prayer is all about. In our earliest version in Mark, we are left in no doubt about Jesus' personal agony. Mark writes: '[Jesus] began to be greatly distressed and troubled. And he said to [his disciples], "My soul is very sorrowful, even to death; remain here, and watch." And going a little further, he fell on the ground and prayed' (Mark 14.34–35 RSV).

But could the perfect human being, the man who lived in perfect obedience to his heavenly Father, really display such inner turmoil? How could he be a model for us, unless he showed an altogether different spirit, one which demonstrated that he had got beyond struggle and conflict, one which showed his life of prayer as one of unclouded vision, living in humble and complete acceptance of whatever his Father planned for him? In all probability, it was questions such as these that Luke put to himself, and which led him to omit all Mark's references in these verses to Jesus' troubled soul. Indeed, so determined is Luke to present a different picture, that so far from Jesus 'throwing' himself in agony upon the ground, he merely 'withdrew from them a stone's throw, and knelt down and prayed' (Luke 22.41 RSV). Perhaps inevitably, many famous paintings of the incident – such as those of El Greco or Bellini – have followed suit, and so we see nothing of the internal agony of Christ, so prominent in Mark's account.

Nor is this transformed presentation confined in Luke to Christ; the behaviour of the disciples is also pushed towards more positive conceptions. Whereas Mark's version of Peter's denial makes no acknowledgement of his future good work (14.29–31), in Luke's version the denial is actually introduced by a more positive prediction: 'Simon, Simon, behold, Satan demanded to have you, that he might sift you like wheat, but I have prayed for you that your faith may not fail; and when you have turned again, strengthen your brethren' (22.31–32 RSV). Astonishingly, even the motivation for the disciples falling asleep is changed. In Mark it is simply because 'their eyes were very heavy' (v. 40); in other words, they were very tired. Luke by contrast insists that they were 'sleeping for sorrow' (v. 45). He thus equally makes the disciples everywhere conform to the sanitized view of prayer. Whereas in Mark they are struggling, and it is unclear where that struggle will lead, in Luke they have become a very different model for us – yes, still weak, but a weakness that is guaranteed to issue in strength because their commitment, their obedience, their willingness to say, 'Thy will be done' is already there.

However, the toing and froing between the two different versions of prayer is still not at an end. For there remains two further verses in Luke (43–44) to be considered, which point in a very different direction from the rest of his narrative: 'And there appeared to him an angel from heaven, strengthening him. And being in an agony he prayed more earnestly, and his sweat became like great drops of blood falling down upon the ground' (RSV). In some modern translations you will find that these words are either deleted entirely or merely printed as a footnote. The explanation is that many scholars regard them as not original to the text, and that seems to me exceedingly likely in view of what I have already said about Luke's general position. Certainly they are being quoted as early as the second century in Justin Martyr, who gives his source something called 'the memoirs of the apostles', but their absence from some of our best manuscripts, including the Codex Vaticanus, makes it much more likely that it is some later editor who has incorporated into Luke's account their powerful and moving image of our Lord sweating great drops of blood.

This supposition would seem confirmed by the fact that in the third century neither of the two great Alexandrian theologians, Clement and Origen, display any knowledge of the two verses being in Luke, despite the fact that they could have been used to provide highly effective ammunition for their general account of prayer, an account that very much veers towards the notion of its all-inclusive, non-sanitized character: as a struggling or wrestling with God and his purposes for us. For it is they who launch the Church upon a particular reading of Genesis 32 – Jacob's wrestling with the angel – which takes the story as the model of precisely what prayer is all about.

Historians of religion tell us that almost certainly at its start no more was involved in this tale than the patriarch wrestling with the local guardian spirit of the place, and because of his perseverance thereby acquiring some entitlement to the land round about Peniel. However, for subsequent Christian tradition it says so much more: it speaks of our need to wrestle in prayer with all the ills, evils, and uncertainties that challenge us, in the knowledge that it is only through such wrestling, such agonizing that we will then be enabled to find the object of our encounter transformed – no longer something threatening, but God himself there at the end of the process to welcome and bless us.

The greatest of Charles Wesley's poems is dedicated to this theme, and perhaps nowhere else is that struggle, that wrestling in prayer and its eventual resolution, more powerfully captured. A few lines will suffice:

> Come, O thou Traveller unknown
> Whom still I hold, but cannot see,
> My company before is gone,
> And I am left alone with thee,
> With thee all night I mean to stay,
> And wrestle till the break of day.

154

I need not tell thee who I am,
My misery, or sin declare

. . . .
Wrestling I will not let thee go,
Till I thy name, thy nature know.

'Tis Love, 'tis Love! Thou died'st for me,
I hear the whisper in my heart
The morning breaks, the shadows flee;
Pure Universal Love thou art;

. . . .
My prayer hath power with God; the Grace
Unspeakable I now receive,

. . . .
In vain I have not wept, and strove,
Thy nature and thy name is Love.

My conclusion should now be clear. Tempting though it is to suppose that we must always present our best face to a being as holy and pure as God, such an attitude is quite mistaken. Despite the depth and profundity of Luke's Gospel in general, here at least he went wrong. It is every aspect of ourselves that we need to expose to God in our prayers – our worries, our ambitions, our desires. For only then can his healing power begin to take effect, and we too be given a vision like that of Jacob at Jabbok's brook, at Peniel.

30 ✣ Two Men
Called Jesus

—

Now the chief priests and elders persuaded the people to ask for
Barabbas and destroy Jesus

(Matt. 27.20 RSV)

In this meditation I would like to reflect upon the two individuals
called 'Jesus' alluded to in Matthew, chapter 27. With one of them
you are already very familiar, Jesus our Lord, but do not be
alarmed if the second evokes no answering chord in your memory. For unless you possess a Bible that lists alternative manuscript
readings or, like the New English Bible, adds the name 'Jesus' to
the body of the text, there is no reason why you should ever have
encountered the other 'Jesus' (or, at least, under this name). But
in fact at verse 16 some manuscripts inform us that Barabbas' first
name was 'Jesus'. Though the name only occurs in a minority of
the manuscripts, the tradition is almost certainly correct.

Clearly, what happened is that out of reverence for our Jesus
scribes when copying the Gospel were reluctant to use the same
name for the guilty criminal Barabbas, and so omitted his first
name. With the obvious exception of Spanish-speaking Christians,
it is a convention that has been maintained to this day, and so it is
unlikely that any children in England have been baptized with the
name 'Jesus'. By contrast, in first-century Palestine it was in fact a
very popular choice, 'Jesus' simply being the Greek form of the
common Hebrew name 'Joshua'.

There is a further interesting twist in the criminal's name. For
Barabbas literally means, son (*bar*) of a father (*abba*). No doubt,
like most of our surnames, by this time no particular significance

still attached to its original meaning. Even so, it is fascinating to reflect that if we had to find some modern English equivalent, it would turn out to be something like Everyman, since we are all sons or daughters of fathers. So in effect the choice which Pilate offers the crowd at verse 17 is between Jesus the Christ, literally Jesus the one anointed or commissioned by God, and Jesus Everyman, with the former clearly innocent and the latter described as 'a notable criminal'. Indeed, the latter phrase is so non-specific that we might further generalize, and say that the real contrast is simply between innocence and guilt. For, whereas Mark's Gospel informs us of the details of Barabbas' crime, that he had taken part in armed insurrection and murder against the Roman authorities (15.7), Matthew (despite having Mark's text before him) deletes, for whatever reason, all such references, and so we are left with the simple bare contrast of innocence with guilt.

By now you may well be wondering where all this is leading. Atonement, or more literally at-one-ment, is the name we attach to Christian doctrine concerning the significance of Christ's death: what it was in that death which effected our at-one-ment, our reconciliation with God despite the depths of human sin. One popular way of expressing its significance, particularly in some forms of Evangelical Christianity, is to suggest that paralleling the earthly trial there was a heavenly judgement, that on the cross Jesus bore the punishment due to our sins, and so (guilty though we are) we can now go free. We need only repent; no punishment can now await us.

More technically, this is known as the doctrine of penal substitution, and for all I have said to the contrary, you might well suppose that that is precisely the direction in which my comparison of the two men called Jesus must point. However, that is very far from my intention. Penal substitution has two fatal flaws: not only does it postulate an angry God who must punish, whereas Jesus himself teaches a message of forgiveness, it makes God punish the innocent instead of the guilty, a perversion of justice if there ever was one! But this is certainly not to say that reflecting on the earthly trial cannot teach us much about how our reconciliation with God is effected; in fact, it is precisely because I believe there to be a more helpful approach available, one based on that contrast between the two men called Jesus, that I began by drawing your attention to what Matthew does with the contrast.

For it seems to me that, if we are ever to be truly reconciled with God, truly at one with him, we must first identify with the less likely of the two Jesuses, Jesus Barabbas, Jesus Everyman, Jesus the guilty one, and that it is only once we have done this that the other Jesus, Jesus the Christ, Jesus the Anointed One, Jesus the innocent, can then effectively succeed in becoming our Saviour and Deliverer. Let me explain.

Much of Jesus' teaching was concerned not with denouncing sin, but with attempting to evoke a sense of its consciousness in the first place. Recall his despairing comment about the Pharisees: that it is not the healthy that need a doctor, but the sick; in other words, he can only begin to heal those who recognize that there is something wrong with their lives in the first place, not those too self-righteous (like the Pharisees) to concede a problem, and that is no doubt one reason why he addressed his message to prostitutes and collaborators – some of them at least were all too aware of the gravity of the wrong they were doing.

But what was true in Jesus' day remains equally true of our own. We all like to live in a world of self-deception, and to believe ourselves good, or at least much better than the average, and in many respects for most readers that may well be true. But it certainly will not be true in all respects. There are bound to be numerous failures, failures in relations with family, friends, and colleagues at work, failures in being generous to those in need, and so on, and it is only if we unreservedly pronounce ourselves guilty, pronounce ourselves like Jesus Barabbas, 'the guilty one', that we can then turn in confidence to that other Jesus, the physician, the doctor who can now work upon our souls because our resistance to conceding the problem has gone.

And how will the other Jesus do this? First, being himself innocent, by forgiving us upon behalf of all those innocent victims whom we ourselves have wronged – the wife whom we have treated like a door-mat, the colleague at work whom we have taken delight in needling, the child going hungry in the Third World as we hurried by to avoid the rattling collection box, and so on. Again, the potential list is endless. But it is not just a matter of being forgiven the past, of the innocent God upon the cross wiping out the consequences of our past failures. It is also equally a matter of the future.

If Jesus Everyman was our past, Jesus the Anointed One must be our future, not just in the sense of trying to copy his example, but praying that we too may be anointed like him, we too be given the gift of the Spirit to indwell our hearts, so that through God's grace our own transformation may also now be possible. Yet to express it thus for most of us is still not quite right. For, as already noted, Christ means the 'anointed one', the one 'commissioned' by God. But have those of us who are baptized not already received our commission at our baptism? So used are we to taking Romans 6 with its talk of death to sin and rising to life again as our principal clue to the significance of baptism, that we forget that for Jesus himself the experience of baptism must have been very different, being his commissioning by his Father for his public ministry with all that entailed. And did we not also receive our commissioning in our baptism, explicitly symbolized in some denominations and parishes by anointing the child with the oil of chrism? Of course at the time, those of us baptized as children understood little of what was meant, but just as our Lord grew in understanding of his mission, his commission, so can and must we.

There you have the substance of what I want to say: that a key part of what atonement is all about is us moving from recognition of ourselves as we really are, Jesus Barabbas, through forgiveness from Jesus the innocent victim, to beyond, our ultimate destiny as one with Jesus the Anointed, Jesus the one suffused with the holy and loving Spirit of God. It is an identity that began in baptism and that under God's grace will end with us as *alteri Christi* ('other Christs') – our commission now fully sealed and endorsed by our heavenly Father.

31 ✣ Why Me?

—

Jesus, knowing that all was now finished, said (to fulfil the scripture), 'I thirst'

(John 19.28 RSV)

Of all the accounts of our Lord's passion, the one in John's Gospel has on first hearing the least power to move. Jesus proceeds too confidently, too self-assuredly, towards his death. Mark's Jesus is dumb before Pilate like a lamb before its shearers, whereas the governor in John's Gospel is told by Jesus in no uncertain terms that 'you would have no power over me unless it had been given you from above' (19.11 RSV). Again, whereas with Mark's version we are moved to tears with the poignancy of Jesus' cry of dereliction from the cross, 'My God, my God, why have you forsaken me?', in its place there appears to come in John what in the original can only be read as a great cry of triumph. For 'it is finished' is all too weak a translation; it is more like a great shout of joy: 'all has been accomplished' (19.30). Then, to cap it all, John insists that for Jesus even the very moment of his death was under his control. Whereas the other evangelists merely record that Jesus 'gave up the ghost', John adds that 'he bowed his head', and bowing one's head was the one sure-fire way of preventing sufficient oxygen from reaching someone hanging on a cross, and so of hastening death. Then what of the prosaic, 'I thirst', also unique to John? Is any capacity it might have to move us not effectively undermined by the way in which it is introduced, with Jesus saying it 'to fulfil the scripture' and 'knowing that all was now finished' (19.28 RSV)?

WHY ME?

That I suspect is almost everyone's first reaction. But, as so often with the Gospels, there are deeper reserves to be tapped. Once we tap these reserves, what we shall gain is not only a better understanding of the relation between the different evangelists' accounts, but also a profound message for ourselves when we too enter that vale of desolation as it was experienced by our Lord.

The fact that Mark quotes Jesus' cry of dereliction in Aramaic, the everyday language of Palestine at the time, makes it virtually certain that what we have here are the actual words of Jesus. 'Eloi, Eloi, lama sabachthani?' (15.34), writes Mark, though Matthew wisely corrects 'Eloi' to the Hebrew 'Eli' (27.46), since otherwise it is hard to explain why the crowd would have misunderstood it as a cry for Elijah's help. The resultant mixture of languages surely makes all the more poignant Jesus' troubled, confused, tortured state. With these words he enters into all the anxiety, doubt, and perplexity which each of us experiences when suffering first confronts us, and thus – take note – implicitly endorses that experience. Jesus too thus asks the agonized question, 'Why, oh why me?'

As Christians, it is all too easy to be way-laid into thinking that because we have a firm hope for the future, all such uncertainties must be put firmly behind us, with no doubt or grief allowed along the way in the present. Indeed, I have even known clergy to upbraid mourners for showing their grief on the grounds that such sorrow is inappropriate in those who are truly confident of the future of their loved one in Christ. But it would seem to me that in such cases the fault really lies with the priest and not with the mourner. For it is surely an essential part of our finite, temporal condition that we need time, time to come to terms with the new, especially when it is threatening, whether it be the loss of a loved one, or as here, the experience of awful pain. Thus undoubtedly right are those hospital chaplains who urge a very different course of action: that no criticism should be levelled against patients who wish initially to rail against

God when pain first strikes, and thus vent the anguished cry, 'Why me?'

Jesus too entered fully into that anguished cry. He too experienced pain in all its essential arbitrariness. It wasn't as though he had to die upon a cross. Had he lived centuries earlier, and in Greece, he could have experienced the painless punishment of poisoning by hemlock. Centuries later, and it might have been something very much worse, as in our own age when prisoners are tortured for years on end before being tossed into some anonymous grave. And so he too cried: 'Why this? Why me?'

Yet note how he cried. Even as he cries in his doubt and in his uncertainty, he cries: 'My God, my God'. He was in fact quoting the opening verse of Psalm 22, which, despite its opening, finally ends in the words of confident trust. As a result, it is sometimes suggested that Jesus quotes the psalm with this fact consciously in view. But I doubt it. The confusion of Hebrew and Aramaic suggests a troubled soul, grasping at whatever straw came to mind. Even so, precisely because that straw was an appeal to his Father in heaven, that same Father was enabled to help him, and so carry him through and beyond the pain. Nor has Mark any doubt about this. For, though these are the only words he attributes to Jesus on the cross, not only does his Gospel end with Jesus vindicated and the tomb empty, even as he dies we see Jesus transforming the world through his suffering, with the centurion at the foot of the cross acknowledging: 'Truly this was the Son of God', and the Temple curtain rent apart (15.38–39). .

Mark thus leaves us in no doubt of his conviction that though we must begin with that cry 'Why me?', the divine help of God's grace refuses to allow that we end there. For such grace, such divine help, has the power to transform our suffering, to make it redemptive, make it creative both for ourselves and for others. Yet both Luke and John clearly were worried whether the reader would get the point, and so that cry of dereliction is omitted. In its place in Luke comes only the final calm acceptance: 'Father, into thy hands I commit my spirit' (23.46 RSV), a pattern which may initially seem to be simply repeated in John with his 'It is finished'. However, there is more to observe just beneath the surface, and it is with that more that I wish to end.

Of all the evangelists, John is the one who takes the most liberties with historical fact. For him, nothing must be allowed to stand in the way of conveying the gospel as the 'good news' it is. After all, what matters is not the details of what happened, but what it signified, what it can tell us that will bring new life and liberation to us. So, for instance, whereas the other evangelists inform us that Maundy Thursday was a Passover meal, John makes the crucifixion happen on the Day of Preparation for the Passover (19.14). The result is that we can envisage Jesus dying as the lambs are being slaughtered in the Temple, and so see him as himself our Passover lamb, as the one who, like those first Passover lambs in Egypt, will deliver us from all that oppresses us and makes us less than fully human, including the awfulness of pain. And just in case we failed to get the point the first time round, a few verses later (v. 29) we are even told that the vinegar Jesus was offered to drink was stretched up to him, not on a lance as in the other Gospels, but on 'hyssop', the very thing used to sprinkle the blood of the Passover lambs on the lintels of the Israelites' doors as they received their liberation from God (Exod. 12.22).

Likewise, John's words for Jesus on the cross should not read as mere history; we need to look beneath to see the good news, the significance that John intends to convey by them. What we then find is John deepening Mark's point: that it was God himself who entered into that cry of dereliction, God himself who wrought the pain's creative transformation, and God who is now available in the here and now to effect that transformation for us.

It was perhaps not altogether an implausible inference on the part of John to deduce that the soldiers' offer of vinegar to Jesus was in response to a cry of thirst, but whether so or not, the reason for recording it lies almost totally elsewhere. In chapter 4, Jesus had identified himself as 'living water' such that 'whoever drinks' of it 'will never thirst' (4.7–15). Then in chapter 7, he went further: 'out of his heart shall flow rivers of living water' (v. 38 RSV). Yet here now in chapter 19 we have the very source of living water, God himself, thirsting: completely entering into our condition at its most basic need. But entering it to transform it, and transform it permanently. For John's 'it is finished' is in Greek what is called a perfect tense, and so means not just that something *has* been accomplished, but equally *is* being accomplished in the present. Even without the resurrection, John is telling us, the cross itself can become a victory, and thus so too can our own sufferings, our own worries, our own doubts. For God himself is alongside us in all of them, not only as the fellow-sufferer who understands, but also offering us help in transforming the suffering, worries, and doubts. It is God who gives us the power to stop our sorrows from eating away at us; it is he who gives us the healing peace and courage with which to face them; it is he who enables us to learn from them, and to stretch beyond them to others who also stand in need of God's love. How far any particular human being can do this is not of course for us to judge. All we know for certain is that God's aid is there: sometimes to achieve little, sometimes much.

One final thought. John alone records that 'blood and water' flowed from Christ's side (19.34), the blood of death and the water of life together flowing there as one; the death of the cry, 'My God, my God, why me?' blossoming into the triumphant shout of 'All is accomplished'. One's thirst, one's agony, can indeed become waters of life both for oneself and for others if only we but let the suffering God recreate us in his own image.

32 ❖ Torn Curtains

—

In the body he was put to death, in the spirit he was raised to life,
and, in the spirit, he went to preach to the spirits in prison
(1 Pet. 3.18–19 JB)

All of us have family and friends without explicit religious belief,
and so the question of what is to happen to them after death
cannot but sometimes raise itself in our minds. Indeed, it is a
question which has become all the more intense in our modern
world, as we become increasingly and embarrassingly aware that
compared with the rather jaded sentiments of some of our fellow
Christains, it is adherents of other faiths who display the deeper
and more profound religious commitment. Even so, in response
we are frequently told that the New Testament gives an unequivocal answer: 'there is salvation in no one else, for there is no other
name under heaven given among men by which we must be
saved' (Acts 4.12 RSV); 'If a man does not abide in me, he is cast
forth as a branch and withers' (John 15.6 RSV). But to me that
seems a very superficial reading. To see why, let me begin by
taking you on a conducted tour of the Temple in Jerusalem in
Jesus' day.

The building is in fact the third, and most magnificent so far.
The first had been erected by Solomon in the tenth century BC,
but this had been destroyed by the Babylonians when they in-
vaded the southern kingdom of Judah in 587 BC. A second one
had then been erected at the instigation of the prophets Haggai
and Zechariah in 520, but, not long before the birth of Christ, this
too had been demolished at the instigation of Herod the Great.

He had decided to build something more impressive, mainly as a means of trying to gain popularity for his regime, which was of doubtful legality.

The basic plan, however, remained essentially the same throughout these rebuildings. First, there is a large Outer Court, to which Gentiles are admitted, and that, I'm afraid, is as far as you or I may go on pain of death. Then there follows a succession of inner courts, each marking the furthest point to which someone in that particular category may proceed. Thus next comes the Women's Court, the furthest point of access for female Jews; next the Court of the Israelites, the furthest point of access for male Jews who are not priests; and then finally the Priests' Court, with its many outside altars, and from these the Temple itself is at last fully visible – a small rectangular structure, 90 feet long, 90 feet high, and 30 feet wide.

Inside the Temple there is then a further division, the larger part being taken up with what is known as the Holy Place, and the smaller remaining third with what is known as the Holy of Holies, at the far end of the building. The latter is separated from the former by a double curtain so that it is impossible to see inside the Holy of Holies from the Holy Place. All one can see are the two ornaments which stand in front of these curtains.

First, there is a rather fine seven-branched lampstand, made of solid gold, known as the menorah, which we learn from the Triumphal Arch of Titus in the Roman Forum was so heavy that it would have taken eight men to lift. But it was by no means intended to be purely ornamental. The lights on it continually burn, since they are in fact the only source of light in the building, the Temple having neither windows nor roof lights. Then there is also an altar upon which incense continually burns, and here too the objective is not just decorative. For when one thinks of all that meat being butchered for sacrifice just outside the doors, and of the way in which meat so quickly smells in hot climates, you can appreciate how necessary all that incense in fact was!

The smaller section of the building, the Holy of Holies, was in fact entered only once a year by the High Priest on the Day of Atonement, Yom Kippur, when on behalf of the people he sprinkled blood on a slab of gold, called the Mercy Seat, as a symbol of their penitence and desire for reconciliation with God. Beneath this Mercy Seat had originally been placed the wooden Ark of the Covenant, with which the presence of God had been traditionally particularly associated, and which had accompanied the people during their wanderings in the desert, but this had been destroyed at the time of the Babylonian invasion.

Such then was the form of worship under the Old Covenant, with everything done to emphasize the difficulty of access to God – his frightening, awesome majesty, so awesome that the place he is felt to be most fully present, the Holy of Holies, may be approached only after the most elaborate preparations, and then on only one day of the year, and by one person, the High Priest of the time, who will have had a lifetime of preparation for this most solemn act.

And then when he does pass beyond the Veil, beyond the double curtain, what does the High Priest discover? Gold, the symbol of majesty and splendour; but because of the absence of windows, there is a darkness so deep the gold can scarcely be observed. Yes, there would almost certainly have been awe, but God's presence must also have been felt as dark, brooding, and threatening.

Given the centrality of such imagery to the Judaism of the time, it should occasion us no surprise that the New Testament writers are quick to use the abolition of these divisions as a metaphor for the transformation which can be wrought by Christ in our lives. Christ as our High Priest permanently entering the Holy of Holies on our behalf is the central theme of the epistle to the Hebrews, while Ephesians declares Christ to be the source of peace between Jew and Gentile because it is he who 'has broken down the dividing wall of hostility' (2.14 RSV). But the verse with which we are most likely to be familiar is the one in Mark that immediately

167

follows Christ's death: 'And the curtain of the Temple was torn in two, from top to bottom' (15.38 RSV). Given, as already noted, the inaccessibility of those curtains, it is hard to see how Jesus' followers could ever have known that this had happened. So in all probability what we have here is a phenomenon by no means unknown in contemporary preaching – a vivid sermon illustration taken literally! And what a magnificent sermon it must have been! For one could scarcely have more concisely and more effectively characterized the liberating power of Christ. God is no more distant, no more to be feared; he is here in our midst to bring life, healing and salvation to all.

But if that is so, can it be our place once more to re-erect barriers, re-erect walls, have once more curtains of division? It is not impossible that even as he wrote this verse, Mark thought so. For immediately following comes the conversion of the pagan centurion, and thus juxtaposed it is all too easy to read Mark as saying that with those torn curtains God is simply saying 'No' to the Judaism of the past and 'Yes' to the Gentile Christianity of Mark and his own community. Anyway, whether fair or not, Matthew feels that this possible reading needs correction, and it is with that correction and its implications for the non-Christian dead that I wish to draw these thoughts together.

The smaller of Matthew's alterations is that no more does the centurion alone confess Jesus as the Son of God, but all 'those who were with him, keeping watch' (27.54 RSV). Jew as much as Gentile is thus allowed to make the definitive pronouncement. However, more substantially, not only is the curtain torn but 'the tombs also were opened, and many bodies of the saints who had fallen alseep were raised, and coming out of the tombs . . . appeared to many' (52–53 RSV). More often than not commentators dismiss all this as no more than legendary accretions. Certainly, it is hard to make any historical sense of it. For, to put it crudely, once raised from the dead, what was to happen to them? Was their post-resurrection life to follow the pattern of Christ's and, if so, why them and not others?

The truth would seem to be that once more we have a piece of symbolism, which Matthew has presented literally. Yet that in no way means that it is, patronizingly, to be dismissed. For not only is it a marvellous piece of symbolism, but it revolutionizes Mark's point; and that gives us an answer to our own present dilemmas about those who die outside the fold of the Christian faith. The torn curtains offer a message of hope and liberation for those who have died as faithful Jews no less than for those who die in the faith of Christ. Because in life they have responded as best they could (they are 'saints', 'holy people', Matthew tells us), in death, as Jesus goes to join them, there he finds a welcoming, answering chord. The torn curtain tears even the divisions of death.

It was to express that conviction that there first entered into the Apostles' Creed the phrase: 'he descended into hell'. For though later the stress had changed, and the notion of the harrowing of hell, of Christ at his death routing Satan, came to be seen as central, its earlier message was one of hope for the non-Christian dead; and it is that view which we find reflected not only here in Matthew, but also in 1 Peter 3.18–20. This latter passage indeed goes further than Matthew. For not only is Christ envisaged as preaching to the saintly dead, even those who failed to obey at the time of Noah are given a second chance. Presumably the author finds it impossible to believe – as we do – that there could only have been eight people in the whole world willing *ever* to say 'Yes' to God, though that is all, according to Genesis 7.13, that were allowed to survive the Flood.

One final thought. If all this seems far too reassuring, and effectively to blunt the challenge of the gospel, let me remind you that nowhere does the New Testament speak of all being saved; indeed, it seems to assume very much the opposite. So even though the message of the crucifixion is of the gates of heaven thrown open to all, it by no means follows that all will want to enter. The challenge remains: has what has been thought and done on earth made their hearts, our hearts, able to give a willing response?

33 ✤ On
Not Clinging

—

The disciples did not know that it was Jesus
(John 21.4 RSV)

Reflect for a moment on the most intimate of human relationships, parents and children, wife and husband, or close friends. In
all such cases, I am sure you will agree, one of the most difficult
lessons to learn is that intimacy and closeness are not at all the
same thing. To see the point, one need only consider the
smothering effect of some marriages or parenting – the husband
surprised by his wife walking out on him because he always assumed that her wishes coincided with his own, or the parent
disconcerted by a child now grown to adulthood and deeply re-
sentful of having been forced into grooves not of his or her choosing. Closeness there certainly had been, but no intimacy; no
proper recognition of the other's essential otherness, or the quest
to discover what really makes them tick.

This is an observation which applies not just to the mother
who badgers her daughter into being the doctor she herself
always wanted to be, or the ham-fisted son forced to mimic
his father's enthusiasm for sport, it is also true of those who
once listened but now no longer do so. Even more insidious
perhaps is the trap into which we are all in danger of falling: of
supposing that there is nothing more to learn about the others
to whom we are most closely related. For, because we all change
and develop, it is precisely at this point, when we think we know
it all, that marriages begin to dissolve and friendships come
under strain.

Paradoxically, then, it is by keeping a certain distance from those we love, by always acknowledging their otherness as a person, that true intimacy is most likely to be achieved. It is a lesson which the disciples too had to learn. Jesus had called them his friends, but like all friends they found it hard to see Jesus in any terms but their own: the local boy from Nazareth made good, certainly called to a unique role as God's Messiah, but still essentially one of themselves – a Galilean accent, knowledgeable about carpentry and fishing, mother and brothers still alive, and so forth. It would clearly require something dramatic to knock them into a new level of perception as to who Jesus really was.

That knock, that jolt, was the resurrection. One of the more intriguing aspects of the various incidents we have recorded is the failure of the disciples immediately to recognize Jesus. People have no trouble with ghosts; so why any difficulty with Jesus? Surely it was because he was not a ghost, but someone who had entered a new order of reality, and the disciples were now seeing him in that new dimension for the first time. Here was no more God's representative, but in effect God himself. 'All authority in heaven and on earth has been given to me', declares Matthew's risen Christ (28.18 RSV), while in John's Gospel, Thomas can only declare, 'My Lord and my God' (20.28 RSV). But, precisely because he is now recognized for what he had in fact been all along, God incarnate, the evangelists are equally insistent that in the process of recognition nothing of that past should be denied. So all four insist upon the empty tomb: that it is all of his humanity that has been carried up into this present disclosure of his divinity. The divine radiance still eats and drinks with them.

Indeed, so obviously physical is that presence that Mary Magdalene, once she recognizes her Lord, does not want to let him go. She grasps him in longing embrace, and Jesus has to tell her to 'stop clinging to me' (John 20.17, my translation). Many translations just talk about touch, but the Greek is in fact much stronger. Now that she has found her Lord again, Mary wants to keep him with her for ever, to cling to him. So she too had to learn this lesson: that closeness and intimacy are not at all the same thing. Jesus tells her that she must let go because he has 'not yet ascended to the Father' (John 20.17 RSV). The intimacy she sought was to come not by him remaining on earth, but distancing himself from earth, so that a true intimacy, a true closeness, could at last be for ever permanently possible, permanently available, not just for Mary but for us as well.

This permanent availability is in fact one of the great themes of John's Gospel. Almost certainly the last of the Gospels to be written, whoever wrote it has clearly reflected profoundly and deeply on what it might mean to say that Jesus still has significance for us, though he is no longer physically here with us on earth; and it is for this reason, scholars believe, that the 'feel' of John's Gospel is very different from the other three, so determined is its author to convey the permanent significance of Jesus, now disclosed by the resurrection, and not just as the disciples had inadequately understood him during his earthly life. Whether John himself or someone who has reflected at his feet, what the author of this Gospel in effect does is produce a series of sermon-like meditations on that theme, developing and expanding upon the historical Jesus' own words. The Jesus of the Synoptic Gospels almost never talked about himself, whereas John's Christ constantly does so, not because John wishes to deceive, but because therein is contained the truth of the resurrection and the continuing of the life of Christ, as John and his community experience it. So, for instance, the historical Jesus offered a parable of the shepherd's care for the lost sheep (Luke 15.3–7); John's Gospel rightly presses this a stage further to the recognition that by his life Jesus showed himself to be that good shepherd (10.1–18). But not just the good shepherd, the way, the truth, the life, the true vine, the bread of life, and so on, each of these 'I am' saying focusing around the pivotal declaration that 'before Abraham was, I am' (8.58 RSV).

The historical Jesus had twice attacked his fellow Jews for over-reliance on being children of Abraham, in the parable of the rich man and Lazarus (Luke 16.19–31) and in his promise to the

Gentile centurion that he would sit down to feast with Abraham before those who presumptuously assume that they are already 'children of the kingdom' (Matt. 8.5–13). This is the basis upon which John builds his dialogue in chapter 8 (31–59). The details need not concern us here, but its climax certainly should. For in the claim that Christ antedates Abraham (v. 58), it is hard not to detect an allusion to Exodus 3.14, to God's revelation of himself at the Burning Bush as the great 'I am that I am'. But, whether so or not, what clearly Christ is made to claim here for himself is that he is the source of all existence, all life. All those appeals to birth and tradition upon which his contemporaries so obviously relied are now at an end; instead of an impersonally mediated relationship with God, what is now on offer is the possibility of intimate personal communion with God through Christ as the source of all existence, all life. He has come that we may 'have life, and have it abundantly' (10.10 RSV).

It is that same theme that John also takes up in his understanding of 'eternal life'. Once more, central to his aim is to ensure that his readers perceive Jesus not as some past reality, however distinguished, but as the one who can be close to them in the here and now, and so enable them to lead a totally new quality of life. Certainly he did not wish to exclude a future reference for Jesus' promises (e.g. 5.25–29); but what worried him was an excessive placing of all one's expectations and hopes in the future, and so he expands and develops the already existing references of Jesus to eternal life in the synoptics (e.g. Matt 19.16), to bring out what they already imply: that eternal life can indeed begin in the here and now. So throughout his Gospel, eternal life as a present reality is promised in and through Christ: 'My sheep hear my voice . . . and I give them eternal life' (10.27–28 RSV). Note that this is not a future tense; that quality of life, that promised release from all the burdens of our past, is available right now in a personal relationship with Christ.

And so to our conclusion, and with it a return to those resurrection appearances. Though Luke shares with John the mysterious character of Christ's appearing and the disciples' initial lack of recognition, he adds one touch, which may be significant. Our Lord disappears almost as mysteriously as he appears, though where he was known was in 'the breaking of the bread' (Luke 24.35 RSV). Might the evangelist not be suggesting that we can run the same risk as Mary Magdalene: that, if we concentrate on our 'highs' of conscious relation with Christ, whether this be in the Eucharist or elsewhere, we too run a similar risk? In trying to cling to Christ when we are most conscious of him, we will lose that greater closeness, greater intimacy that comes from the realization that he is with us *always*, there in our hearts, whether we are aware of him or not, conforming us to his image, if we will but let him. As the very last words of Matthew's Gospel put it: 'lo, I am with you always, even unto the end of the world' (Matt. 28.20 AV). His distancing himself from us has brought with it the possibility of permanent intimacy – provided, that is, we do not repeat Mary's error of wanting him to be just as he was on earth, or just as we feel we already best know him.

34 ✤ The Beat
at the World's Heart

—

When [Judas] had gone out, Jesus said, 'Now is the Son of Man
glorified'

(John 13.31 RSV)

The Prologue to John's Gospel gives it a marvellously profound
and mysterious opening. Borrowing language used elsewhere of
wisdom, it is intended to express the complete metaphysical identity of Jesus with God; and, as such, it effectively prepares the
reader for the presentation of Jesus' life and significance which is
to follow. However, in our concern to identify Jesus with God we
must not lose sight of the practical thrust which John also has in
mind. That practical thrust contains an even more astonishing
claim, which, if we give it heed, will transform both our perception of the world and our life of discipleship.

Let us begin by asking what it means to say that Jesus is the
divine Word or Logos. Scholars continue to debate the relative
degrees of influence on John of Jewish and Greek modes of
thought. However, increasingly, Greek influence even within Palestine itself is being acknowledged; and in any case, whatever was
determinative for John, as soon as his Gospel became more widely
available in the ancient world, both the Hebrew and the Greek
resonances of the word would inevitably come to play their part.

For the Jewish way of thinking, 'expression' might be a better
translation. For the point is that for each of us – at least in so far as
we tell the truth – our words, what we say, reveal who we essentially are. They express our being. Little wonder, then, that
since God always speaks the truth, his words came to be seen as

completely identified with him, particularly as they are to be found in the Torah or Law (the first five books of the Bible). But, says John, a far better clue to who God is, to the divine expression, is now to be found, not as he is expressed in these words of the Old Testament, but in the very person of a particular individual, this man Jesus.

To that, the Greek understanding of Logos then adds a further dimension. It is not just a matter of Jesus being the perfect expression of God, the guide to who he is; he is also the clue to the world's intelligibility, to its very meaning. The normal Greek for 'to give an account or explanation' of something is *didonai logon*, and by the time of Christ, Logos was being widely used in Stoic and Platonic philosophy, including works of the Jewish philosopher Philo, as a semi-technical term for an underlying principle which could give such intelligibility, make sense of our world.

So John's Gospel opens with a very large claim indeed. Jesus is not only the very expression of God, he is the indispensable clue to making sense of ourselves and the world about us. Indeed, to drive his point home, John deliberately models the opening phrases of his Gospel on the Greek version of Genesis 1; like Genesis 1, he portrays a Word that triumphs over darkness to bring light. But how can such large claims be substantiated? How is the light to dawn for us, the meaning of the world to become transparent?

Anyone comparing John with the Synoptic Gospels is immediately struck by the extraordinary difference between them in their portrayal of Jesus' consciousness, and on a superficial reading it would be very easy to conclude that with John the humanity disappears altogether, so confidently does Jesus continually speak of his special status as that around which all else revolves. What has happened is that whereas the other evangelists tell us, roughly speaking, how it happened, how Jesus' life culminated in a recognition of his divinity – the being to whom all power on heaven and earth has been given (Matt. 28.18) – John chooses to make the same point in exactly the opposite way. Whereas for the others, to put it a bit crudely, their narratives all ascend towards this climactic disclosure, with the benefit of hindsight John chooses instead a pattern of descent, away from his starting point in unqualified dignity and power. In other words, while the narratives of Matthew, Mark, and Luke build up (with some hints along the way) towards a climactic disclosure of Jesus' full significance as divinity in our midst, John's opening chapter already leaves us in no doubt; instead of the synoptic narratives of a humanity gradually revealed to be so much more, in John we now have one of divinity willing to become so much less – one of ourselves. This descent in place of ascent is there in order to shock us into recognition of what this life of Jesus can truly say to us, not only about the meaning of our own lives, but about the very meaning of the universe itself.

For me, the most effective way in which John does this is through his use of one of his favourite words, glory. The Hebrew word literally means 'weight', and so in a human context it describes whatever makes us feel the weight of other people's presence, and so it is used, for instance, of the wealth of Abraham and Jacob (Gen. 13.2; 31.1) as also of the worldly honours accorded Joseph in Egypt (Gen. 45.13). When applied to God, our English Bibles now speak instead of his 'glory' rather than of his 'wealth' and 'splendour', but it is sometimes hard to tell the difference. It is basically still, more often than not, just a demonstration of brute power (e.g. Ps. 97.1–6), of human beings feeling the 'weight' of the divine presence.

But John changes all that. Not for him the weight of power, the weight of wealth, but glory in descent, glory even in humiliation. Thus at the pivotal point of his Gospel when Judas goes off to betray Jesus, John makes Jesus say: 'Now is the Son of Man glorified, and in him God is glorified' (13.31 RSV). Though occasionally the Synoptics use the phrase 'Son of Man' of an exalted figure (e.g. Mark 14.62), there seems little doubt that John means something quite different here. He borrows the sense of the term from its normal use on the lips of Jesus, who had used it to speak of

177

himself as the Son of Man destined to suffer, and it is that representative, suffering humanity with which John identifies the divine glory elsewhere.

But of course it was not pointless suffering. The cross is where a life of obedience to his Father had led, a life of obedient love. Like this transformed glory, love is a repeated theme in John: chapter 3: 'For God so loved the world that he gave his only Son' (v. 16); chapter 13: 'Having loved his own . . . he loved them to the end' (v. 1); chapter 15: 'Greater love has no man than this, that a man lay down his life for his friends. You are my friends' (vs. 13–14 RSV). Again and again, John drives home his theme: that love and glory go together. God's weight lies in his love; God's glory lies in his willingness to suffer for that love.

The Prologue ends with the declaration that 'the Word became flesh and dwelt among us . . . and we have beheld his glory' (1.14 RSV). The Logos, the divine expression, the clue to the world's intelligibility, hangs on a cross, with all the weight, all the splendour, all the glory of divinity focused in that act of love. It is thus not ostentation or power that lie at the world's real heart, but the gentle beat of the heart of love upon that cross. Listen to its quiet murmur, and the perception of your life and your understanding of the very world itself will be totally transformed. Why not let the revolution begin now?

✢ Conclusion ✢
Spreading the Gospel

35 ✤ *Head*
in the Clouds

—

A cloud took him out of their sight
(Acts 1.9 RSV)

When we want to describe someone who is out of touch with reality, we talk of them having their 'head in the clouds'. If a survey were to be conducted to determine where traditional Christian belief is most out of touch with reality, the ascension, I suspect, would come fairly high on most people's list. Christ zooming like a rocket up into the heavens – what possible significance could that have? Yet it seems to me that, so far from being peripheral, what it implies lies at the very heart of the Christian faith. Not only that: by the end of this meditation, I hope to have persuaded you that it is precisely by endorsing talk of a head in the clouds that its full significance can be best appreciated.

Though there are a number of allusions elsewhere, for instance in John and in Ephesians, it is only Luke who provides us with a description, and indeed almost certainly with two: one at the end of his Gospel and the other at the beginning of Acts. For, though some manuscripts omit 'and he was carried up into heaven' (Luke 24.51 RSV) from the Gospel account, Acts seems to imply its presence, since it begins with a resumé, declaring that Luke in his Gospel had already described 'all that Jesus began to do and teach until the day when he was taken up' (Acts 1.1–2 RSV). What stands in the way of such an identification is that we would then have two accounts of the ascension, differing in detail and assuming a different chronology. Yet to raise that objection is to yield to the modern pedantry for historical accuracy and to forget that the ancient world had rather different standards. For what surely concerned Luke more was to convey the significance of what had happened; and, measured by that criterion, conflicting details pale into the trivia they really are.

So to start worrying about whether or not forty days elapsed between Jesus' resurrection and ascension (Acts 1.3) is to miss Luke's real point, which is either a rough biblical number or, more probably, symbolic. For forty played a key role in the life of Moses and Elijah: Moses was forty years in the wilderness; Elijah forty days in the desert before his definitive experience at the cave on Mount Horeb, where he heard 'the still small voice' (1 Kings 19.4–13). And there seems no doubt that Luke is concerned to relate the ascension to these two great figures of the past.

Thus if we turn back to the transfiguration, it is here, in the disciples' visionary experience of Jesus transfigured in the presence of these two Old Testament heroes, that we have Luke's first reference to the ascension. for when the text speaks of them talking to Jesus about 'his departure which he was to accomplish in Jerusalem' (9.31 RSV), an odd word is used – in Greek, 'exodus'. That might of course refer to his death, but the ascension seems more likely, as a few verses later Luke writes, 'when the days drew near for him to be received up, he set his face to go to Jerusalem' (9.51 RSV). This time he uses the same word for 're-ceived up' as the Old Testament had used to describe Elijah's ascension into heaven (2 Kings 2.9–12), just as on the previous occasion the term 'exodus' we particularly associate with Moses. Even so, we are warned that someone very different is now involved. For almost immediately, the discliples ask to call fire down on those who reject them, just as Elijah had done (2 Kings 1.9–10), only to be sternly rebuked by Jesus (Luke 9.55).

There are also other, more important, differences from the two earlier figures, and here at last we come to part of my theme – clouds. Of Moses it was reported merely that after his last encounter with God on Mount Nebo he was buried and 'no man knows the place of his burial to this day' (Deut. 34.6 RSV), while Elijah's ascension was in a whirlwind, not a cloud (2 Kings 2.11). Cloud would have in fact suggested much more to the Jew of Jesus' time than it does for us today. For here we have a reference to the *Shekinah*, the cloud of the divine presence which led the Israelites during their wanderings in the desert. In the Old Testament account of the Exodus, it is a linguistically related word which is used to describe the tent or tabernacle of meeting, and so when at the transfiguration the disciples propose building three 'tents' or 'booths', what they are in effect acknowledging is the reality of that divine presence.

During Moses' lifetime he had spasmodically been allowed to enter that cloud, in order to obtain advice and guidance from God. But, Luke insists, Jesus' relation to the cloud is quite different. The transfiguration is but one small indication of this future status, when he will be permanently part of that cloud. So, not only at the ascension is he taken up into a cloud, into divinity itself, where he now reigns 'at God's right hand' (Acts 2.33, my translation), the promise is that he shall return from there one day 'coming in a cloud with power and great glory' (Luke 21.27 RSV).

But if the clouds tell us of divinity, Luke is equally insistent that it is humanity, our humanity, which now sits enthroned at God's right hand. As you may know, Luke's view that the ascension marks the end of the resurrection appearances contradicts Paul's account of his conversion in 1 Corinthians 15.3–8, where Paul seems to equate Christ's appearance to him on the Damascus Road (though it took place after the ascension), with the disciples' experience of the bodily resurrected Lord. Luke alludes to Paul's conversion no less than three times in Acts; none the less, for him, something vitally important was missing from that vision that only the pre-ascension bodily experiences could fully convey: that the now exalted Lord had carried with him to heaven every aspect of our humanity, including its full bodily significance, transformed though that must be. That is why in his Gospel account Luke insists that just before the ascension Jesus ate with his disciples (Luke 24.41–43), while in the Acts version, no sooner has the ascension taken place than the Lord is called by his human name, Jesus (Acts 1.11); and this is the way he is repeatedly described throughout the subsequent narrative (sixty-eight times).

The reason for Luke's insistence had already been anticipated in his account of the transfiguration. Whereas Moses had always entered the cloud of the divine presence on his own, Jesus is depicted as enabling his disciples also to enter: 'a cloud came and overshadowed them; and they were afraid as they entered the cloud' (9.34 RSV). Peter, James, and John thereby anticipated their own destiny, as also the destiny of all who call Jesus 'Lord'. He it is who has carried our humanity into heaven, and we too can thus enter the cloud of the divine presence, share in his exaltation, if only we trust in him and follow the example he set for us while on earth.

Psalm 68 (vs. 17–18) speaks of God leading a triumphant procession out of the wilderness into the promised land. The author of Ephesians finds in this his model for the significance of the ascension: 'he ascended into the heights with captives in his train' (4.8 NEB). For Luke, we are those captives, those whom Jesus as perfect humanity, our head, can lead into a new exodus, into a new order of existence, one in which we shall share his life with him as 'our head in the clouds'.

It is thus by ceasing to be obsessed with the literal meaning of Scripture, and looking beyond to its symbolism that we discover its true significance and message: how a man with his head in the clouds has become our head, our salvation.

36 ❖ Built by Wind and Fire

—

And suddenly a sound . . . like the rush of a mighty wind . . . and
. . . there appeared to them tongues as of fire
(Acts 2.2–3 RSV)

What are the first impressions that occur to you when asked to
think of wind or fire? My suspicion is that they are most likely to
be negative: the icy blast of a cold winter's day or fire raging
destructively and out of control through a devastated building.
Yet both wind and fire have of course also their positive side – the
warmth of the fireside, the summer's refreshing breeze. In the
ancient world that positive side was more powerful still. The
naked flame offered the only way of cooking; so little wonder that
the story of Prometheus bringing the gift of fire from heaven was
among the most popular of the Greek myths. Again, in Palestine's
rainless summer the moisture-laden winds from the Mediterra-
nean spoke of dewy nights refreshing the crops. So to use wind
and fire as images of God hinted as much at his capacity to give
life, as to bring destruction, purgation, or judgement.

However, as we shall see, we need to bear both in mind, as we
turn to consider the two accounts which the New Testament gives
us of the gift of the Spirit to the Church. The better known of the
two, Acts (2.1–4), mentions both wind and fire, while at first sight
in John's account (20.19–23) neither may seem to appear. But in
fact in declaring that the risen Lord 'breathed on them and said
to them, "Receive the Holy Spirit"' (John 20.22 RSV), wind is
certainly being mentioned, since the word John uses for spirit also
means wind; and indeed, earlier in his Gospel he had already

185

played upon this double sense (3.6–8). Spirit is thus being treated here as a sort of gentle wind or breath.

That background – the way the language functions symbolically – will, I hope, now help you to understand better what it is John and Luke (as the author of Acts) are trying to convey. People sometimes get very worried because we have two different accounts of the giving of the Spirit, and they cannot both be literally correct. Did Jesus first give the Spirit as part of a resurrection appearance, as John implies, or after the ascension, as in Luke's version? But both writers agree that Christ's Spirit is now available to transform the Church, and it is how they understood that transformation which should really concern us.

Consider first the account in Acts. Here the effect is that the gathered assembly of disciples speak in tongues, such that the audience who gather to hear them all understand despite their varied backgrounds – 'devout men from every nation under heaven' is how Luke puts it (Acts 2.5 RSV). However, if we stop there, at the comprehension, we miss the main point. Some evidence suggests that Luke is here modelling his account on contemporary understandings of what happened at Sinai, when the Law was given. There too there had been sound and fire (Exod. 19.16–19), while later tradition not only argued (from Exod. 19.1) that the season was that of Pentecost, but also maintained that at the time each had understood what was delivered because it was in his own language. One version of the text of Exodus 20.18 spoke of the people understanding 'voices', whereas the Revised Standard Version correctly translates: 'The people perceived thunderings'. Now the plausibility of such exegesis need not detain us. Rather, what should is the use to which Luke puts it. For just as the rabbis meant to imply by this account that the Law brought a return of the unity which the Tower of Babel had lost, so Luke is telling us that Christ's Spirit can give us a still greater unity, one that will not only deepen already existing relations among Jews, but extend such bonds far beyond the borders of Israel. That is why that same chapter in Acts ends with an idyllic description of the early apostolic, community life – everyone having 'glad and generous hearts' and sharing 'all things in common' (Acts 2.41–47, my translation).

This sense of unity and mutual responsibility for one another as the gift of the Spirit is something for which Luke had already prepared us with the incident which immediately precedes the giving of the Spirit in his account: the suicide of Judas Iscariot and the subsequent choice of Matthias in his place. Both Matthew and Luke agree that Judas' ill-gotten gains were used to buy a plot of land, and that he met an unnatural death. But there the agreement ends. Matthew detects a sign of repentance (27.3–9), whereas Luke (Acts 1.12–26) uses a rival account which has come down to him to portray how divisive life without the divine spirit really is, and he does so by means of a subtle pun or play on words. Matthias is chosen to take his '*place of service* and apostleship' because 'Judas turned aside, to go to his *own place*' (Acts 1.25, my italics and literal translation). Judas in Luke's version buys the field precisely because he is totally turned in on himself, wants 'his own place', whereas our proper place, Luke is telling us, is as part of community, part of service in a life of mutual interdependency.

Yet how are we to acquire such a sense? John answers that question with what is in effect another play on words. Almost certainly Luke is more accurate than John is about when precisely the Spirit was given, but John wants to include it within his Gospel, and so (quite understandably) he takes a few liberties with history. However, once we probe a bit deeper, what we discover is more liberties still, so concerned is he to make it clear how it is that the Spirit can give to the Christian community this new life. For not content with recording the gift as part of the resurrection appearances, John goes one stage further, and equates it with the very death of Christ. All you will learn from most translations is that after Christ's last words from the cross he 'gave up his spirit' (19.30); but John's Greek is in fact deliberately ambiguous. For the phrase can equally well mean: 'he handed over his spirit'. In other words, the power to build community, John is telling us, comes from that death: from we too leading sacrificial lives like Christ's.

Someone who perceived this connection between Pentecost and sacrifice with perfect clarity was Charles Wesley. His hymn 'O Thou who camest from above, the pure celestial fire to impart' is full of references to sacrifice – 'the mean altar of my heart', 'make the sacrifice complete', and so forth. What you may not know is that it all began as a meditation on a verse from Leviticus: 'Fire shall be kept burning upon the altar continually; it shall not go out' (6.13 RSV). Even to this day, Zoroastrians still follow such a rule, burning costly sandalwood where they can, to symbolize that it is only by giving that we can receive and build, in and through that divine fire.

However, for us as Christians, the point is a still deeper one: we are called not just as individuals, but as part of a community, a community built on the transforming power of wind and fire. John sets before us a community permeated by the breath of Christ's sacrifice; Luke one in which the tongues of fire unite each member in mutual comprehension and compassion. The wind or breath of sacrifice that blows from Christ's cross is thus there to set alight such a fire in us that not only can it purge the dross from our lives, but also transform all our stumblings into a community that is fully bonded and empowered by God's Spirit: one in which by taking responsibility for one another we are thereby enabled to take responsibility for the world.

In comparison with that vision both Luke and John deem historical detail unimportant. If we are to work towards the transformation of our world, do we not need to recover their priorities?

Scripture Index

189

Topic Index

TOPIC INDEX